TUTTLE
PRACTICAL
CAMBODIAN
DICTIONARY

D0964841

TUTTLE
PRACTICAL
CAMBODIAN
DICTIONARY

English–Cambodian
Cambodian–English

DAVID SMYTH
and
TRAN KIEN

CHARLES E. TUTTLE COMPANY
Rutland, Vermont & Tokyo, Japan

Published by the Charles E. Tuttle Company, Inc.
of Rutland, Vermont & Tokyo, Japan
with editorial offices at
2-6 Suido 1-chome, Bunkyo-ku, Tokyo 112

© 1995 by Charles E. Tuttle Publishing Co., Inc.

LCC Card No. 94-60681
ISBN 0-8048-1954-8

First edition, 1995

Printed in Japan

CONTENTS

INTRODUCTION

General

Cambodian or Khmer is the national language of Cambodia. In addition, dialects of Cambodian are spoken by approximately half a million people living in the Mekong Delta region of Vietnam, and there are a further half million speakers in Thailand's northeastern provinces of Surin, Buriram, and Sisaket. In Laos, however, the Cambodian-speaking community is much smaller. As a result of the huge political upheavals in Cambodia and the refugee exodus during the 1970s, there are sizeable emigré communities in both France and the USA.

Cambodian is the most important member of the Mon-Khmer family of languages which are spoken across a wide area of Southeast Asia. Unlike the languages of neighboring Thailand, Laos, and Vietnam, Cambodian is not a tonal language. There are, however, many grammatical similarities between all these languages.

Cambodian is written in a unique script that originated in India. The earliest examples of Cambodian writing are stone inscriptions dating from the beginning of the 7th century. Since then, the shapes of individual letters have undergone considerable changes and a number of additional vowel symbols have been introduced. Today, two distinct styles of printed Cambodian exist: *uk-sor j'ree-ung* and *uk-*

sor mool. The former, 'sloping' style is used in normal printing and is the basis for handwritten style, while the latter, more elaborate 'rounded' letters are used for posters, shop names, book titles, and so on.

uk-sor j'ree-ung	ក	ខ	គ	ឃ	ង
uk-sor mool	ក	ខ	គ	ឃ	ង

Comparison of first five consonants of Cambodian alphabet

Cambodian is written from left to right with no spaces between words. It is similar, although more complex, to the Thai and Lao systems of writing. A striking feature of the Cambodian system is that when two consonants occur at the beginning of a word, the second consonant is written beneath the initial consonant, using a special sub-script form. Another major feature is that each vowel symbol can be pronounced in two ways, the appropriate pronunciation depending upon the preceding consonant. Because of the complexities of the Cambodian system of writing, the French colonial administrators attempted, in a short-lived experiment during the 1940s, to introduce romanized Cambodian both for administrative purposes and for newspapers. Since the overthrow of the Khmer Rouge regime there are signs of official attempts to simplify the writing system.

Pronunciation

This dictionary is intended for the English speaker who needs a source of basic Cambodian vocabulary in an easily understandable romanized form. The English-Cambodian section contains approximately 3,500 words and phrases and the Cambodian-English section, almost 2,000 words. Every entry is given in both romanized Cambodian and Cambodian script.

Cambodian has a number of sounds which do not exist in English and which are difficult to represent accurately without resorting to phonetic symbols familiar only to those who have studied linguistics. The system of transcription used in this dictionary is intended to represent Cambodian as simply as possible for the English speaker. It must be remembered, however, that any system of transcription is only an approximation. Since each entry is given in both romanized transcription and Cambodian script, the user can check his or her pronunciation by asking a native speaker to read the Cambodian script entry. The more serious student will learn to read Cambodian and be able to ignore the romanized entries entirely.

A fair approximation of the Cambodian pronunciation can be achieved by reading the romanized entries as if they were English words. However, the following points regarding the romanization system should first be clarified:

Consonant Clusters

A lot of Cambodian words begin with a consonant cluster; that is, two or more consonant sounds at the beginning of a word. Some consonant clusters, such as *sl* and *kr* are straight-forward, as they are similar to sounds that exist in English. Others, however, such as an *l* sound after a *t*, or an *ng* sound after a *ch*, at first sound very strange to the Western ear. These clusters are marked in the transcription with an apostrophe (e.g., *t'lai*, *ch'nguñ*, *s'rok*, etc.); when pronouncing these words it is important not to insert a short *a* vowel between the two initial consonants. A native speaker can demonstrate this.

Consonants

Most consonants have the same pronunciation as in English, but note the following:

bp   a sharp 'p' sound, somewhere between the English 'b' and 'p' (don't actually pronounce the 'b') e.g., **bpee** *(two)*; **bpairt** *(doctor)*

dt   a sharp 't' sound, somewhere between the English 'd' and 't' (don't actually pronounce the 'd') e.g., **dteuk** *(water)*; **dtou** *(go)*

j   as in 'jump'
e.g., **joo-up** *(meet)*; **jong** *(want)*

g   as in 'get'
e.g., **goy** (customs)

ng   as in 'ring', but note that unlike English, this sound can occur in places other than at the end of a word
e.g., **ra-ngee-a** *(cold)* ; **t'ngai** *(day)*

n'y/ñ   as in 'canyon', but this sound can also occur at the beginning or end of a word. (It is transcribed as *ñ* rather than *n'y* at the end of a word.)
e.g., **n'yum** *(eat)*; **ch'nguñ** *(tasty)*

Vowels

Cambodian vowels are notoriously difficult to romanize, but if you follow the guidelines here, you should be able to produce a reasonable approximation of Cambodian pronunciation.

- *-a* as in 'ago'
  e.g., **la-or** *(good)*
- *-aa* a long 'a' sound similar to the English 'car', 'far', etc.
  e.g., **baan** *(can)*
- *-ai* as in 'Thai'
  e.g., **t'lai** *(expensive); **t'ngai** *(day)*
- *-ao* as in 'Lao'
  e.g., **gao seup** *(ninety)*
- *-ay* as in 'pay'
  e.g., **dtay** *(question word)*
- *-ee* as in 'see'
  e.g., **bpee** *(two)*
- *-eu* similar to the English sound of repugnance 'uugh'
  e.g., **dteuk** *(water);* **meun** *(10,000)*
- *-i* as in 'fin'
  e.g., **ni-yee-ay** *(speak)*
- *-o* a short vowel similar to the English 'long'
  e.g., **dop** *(ten)*
- *-oa* a long 'o' vowel similar to the English 'loan', 'moan', etc.
  e.g., **goan** *(child)*
- *-oo* a long vowel, as in 'boot'

e.g., **poom** *(village)*

-ou   a short vowel, with no equivalent in English

e.g., **dtou** *(go)*; **nou** *(live, be situated at)*

-OO   a short vowel, as in 'cook'

e.g., **yOOp** *(night)*

-u   a short vowel, as in 'run'

e.g., **bprum** *(five)*

Where *h* occurs at the end of the transcription [e.g., **nih** *(this)*, **nah** *(very)*] it indicates that the vowel should be pronounced with a breathy voice.

Acknowledgments

The original inspiration for this work was *Robertson's Practical English-Thai Dictionary* (Charles E. Tuttle Co., Inc., 1969), an unpretentious pocket dictionary which many thousands of Westerners learning Thai have found invaluable. In addition, we happily acknowledge our debt to the meticulous works of recent predecessors in the field of Cambodian lexicography: Judith Jacob, Robert Headley, and Franklin Huffman. A valuable source for contemporary political vocabulary is the *JPRS Khmer-English Glossary*. Seam and Blake's *Phonetic English-Khmer Dictionary*, which appears to have also been influenced by Robertson's English-Thai dictionary, was published while the present work was still in manuscript form, so the present authors were able to benefit from a further source for cross-referencing. Lastly, the authors wish to gratefully acknowledge the grant received from the Research and

Publications Committee of the School of Oriental and African Studies, University of London.

Further study

The following dictionaries and language-learning materials may be of interest to those considering studying Cambodian in greater depth.

Headley, Robert. *Cambodian-English Dictionary* (2 vols). Washington D.C. The Catholic University Press.

Huffman, Franklin E. *Cambodian System of Writing and Beginning Reader*. New Haven and London. Yale University Press. 1970.

Huffman, Franklin E. *Modern Spoken Cambodian*. New Haven and London. Yale University Press. 1970.

Huffman, Franklin E. *Intermediate Cambodian Reader*. New Haven and London. Yale University Press. 1972.

Huffman, Franklin E. and Im Proum. *Cambodian Literary Reader and Glossary*. New Haven and London. Yale University Press. 1977.

Huffman, Franklin E. and Im Proum. *English-Khmer Dictionary*. New Haven and London. Yale University Press. 1978.

Jacob, Judith M. *Introduction to Cambodian*. London. OUP. 1968.

Jacob, Judith M. *A Concise Cambodian-English Dictionary*. London. OUP. 1974.

JPRS. *Khmer/English Glossary*. JPRS-SEA-91-022. 17 September, 1991.

Seam, Ung Tea and Neil French Blake. *Phonetic English-Khmer Dictionary*. Seam and Blake Books. Bangkok. 1991.

Smyth, David. *Colloquial Cambodian*. London. Routledge. 1994.

ENGLISH-CAMBODIAN

A

a, an   moo-ay   មួយ

able *(can)*   baan ... បាន

about *(approximately)*   bpra-hail; bpra-maan   ប្រហែល; ប្រមាណ

    (concerning)   bpee; om-bpee   ពី; អំពី

above   ler   លើ

abroad   grao bpra-dtayh   ក្រៅប្រទេស

absent   meun nou   មិននៅ

accept   dtor-dtoo-ul   ទទួល

accident   kroo-ah t'nuk   គ្រោះថ្នាក់

according (to)   dtaam   តាម

account *(bank)*   gong   កុង

accustomed (to)   t'loa-up   ធ្លាប់

ache   cheu   ឈឺ

    headache   cheu g'baal   ឈឺក្បាល

    stomachache   cheu bpoo-ah   ឈឺពោះ

across   ch'long gut   ឆ្លងកាត់

actor, actress   nay-uk layng   អ្នកលេង

add   roo-um   រួម

addict   n'yee-un   ញៀន

address   dtee lOOm-nou; aa-sai-ya-taan   ទីលំនៅ; អាសយដ្ឋាន

adjust   som-roo-ul   សម្រួល

administer   a-pi-baal; krOOp krorng   អភិបាល; គ្រប់គ្រង

administrator   nay-uk a-pi-baal; nay-uk krOOp krorng   អ្នកអភិបាល; អ្នកគ្រប់គ្រង

admire   gaot   កោត

admission *(price)*   t'lai joal   ថ្លៃចូល

adult   ma-nOOh bpeuñ way   មនុស្សពេញវ័យ

advance (v)   chee-un dtou mOOk   ឈានទៅមុខ

advantage   bpra-yaoch   ប្រយោជន៍

   take advantage of   mee-un bpree-up   មានប្រៀប

advertise   koa-sa-naa   ឃោសនា

advice   yoa-bol   យោបល់

advise   s'nar   ស្នើ

advisor   dtee bpreuk-saa   ទីប្រឹក្សា

afraid   klaich   ខ្លាច

after   grao-ee   ក្រោយ

   after that   roo-ich bpee nOOh   រួចពីនោះ

afternoon *(early)*   ra-see-ul   រសៀល

   (late)   l'ngee-ich   ល្ងាច

afterwards   grao-ee moak   ក្រោយមក

again   dtee-ut; m'dorng dtee-ut   ទៀត ; ម្ដងទៀត

   please say that again   soam ni-yee-ay m'dorng dtee-ut   សូមនិយាយម្ដងទៀត

age   aa-yOO   អាយុ

ago   mOOn   មុន

two years ago   bpee ch'num mOOn   ពីរឆ្នាំមុន

agree (with, to)   yoo-ul bprorm (neung)   យល់ព្រម(នឹង)

agriculture   ga-sa-gum   កសិកម្ម

aid (n)   gaa joo-ay; jOOm-noo-ay   ការជួយ; ជំនួយ

AIDS   ayd; see-daa   អេដស៍; ស៊ីដា

air   aa-gaah   អាកាស

air-conditioner   maa-seen dtra-jay-uk   ម៉ាស៊ីនត្រជាក់

air force   gorng dtoa-up aa-gaah   កងទ័ពអាកាស

airmail letter   som-bot dtaam jerng aa-gaah   សំបុត្រតាម ផ្ញើងអាកាស

airplane   g'bul hoh; yoo-un hoh   កប៉ាល់ហោះ; យន្តហោះ

airport   jom-nort yoo-un hoh; aa-gaah-sa-yee-un-taan   ចំណតយន្តហោះ; អាកាសយានដ្ឋាន

alarm clock   nee-a-li-gaa roa   នាឡិការោទ៍

alcohol *(liquor)*   s'raa   ស្រា

alike   doa-ich k'nee-a   ដូចគ្នា

alive   nou roo-ah   នៅរស់

all   dtay-ung oh   ទាំងអស់

allow   a-nOOñ-n'yaat   អនុញ្ញាត

all right *(agreed)*   yoo-ul bprorm   យល់ព្រម

that's all right   meun ay dtay; k'mee-un ay dtay   មិនអ្វី ទេ; គ្មានអ្វីទេ

almost   jeut (neung); ster dtai   ជិត(នឹង);ស្ទើរតែ

almost everyone   ster dtai dtay-ung oh k'nee-a   ស្ទើ រតែទាំងអស់គ្នា

alone m'nay-uk aing ម្នាក់ឯង

along dtaam តាម

alphabet uk-sor អក្សរ

already hai-ee; roo-ich hai-ee ហើយ; រួចហើយ

also dai ដែរ

always jee-a neuch; jee-a dor-raap ជានិច្ច; ជាដរាប

amazed goo-a ch'ngol គួរឆ្ងល់

ambassador *(of a kingdom)* aik-uk-kee-a-ree-ich- a-dtoot
ឯកអគ្គរាជទូត .

   (of a republic) aik-uk-kee-a-roa-ut-ta-dtoot
ឯកអគ្គរដ្ឋទូត

ambulance roo-ut-yoo-un song-kroo-ah រថយន្តសង្គ្រោះ

America aa-may-rik អាមេរិក

American a-may-ri-gong អមេរិកាំង .

among nou k'nong នៅក្នុង

amount jom-noo-un ចន្លួន

ancient bo-raan បុរាណ

and neung និង

anger gom-heung កំហឹង

Angkor Wat ung-gor woa-ut អង្គរវត្ត

angry keung ខឹង

animal sut សត្វ

ankle gor-jerng កជើង

announce bpra-gaah ប្រកាស

annoyed tOOñ ធុញ

it's very annoying tOOñ nah ធុញ្ញាណាស់

another moo-ay dtee-ut មួយទៀត

answer (v) ch'lar-ee; dtorp ឆ្លើយ; តប

ant s'ra-maoch ស្រមោច

any klah ខ្លះ

anyone nor-naa នរណា

anyone will do nor-naa gor baan នរណាក៏បាន

anything a-way; a-way a-way អ្វី; អ្វី ៗ

anything will do a-way a-way gor baan អ្វី ៗ ក៏បាន

anywhere ai naa ឯណា

anywhere will do ai naa gor baan ឯណាក៏បាន

apartment p'dtay-ah l'wairng ផ្ទះល្វែង

apologize som dtoah សុំទោស; សូមទោស

appendicitis roak ra-lee-uk k'naing bpoo-ah wee-un
រោគរលាកខ្នែងពោះវៀន

apply (for) duk bpee-uk ដាក់ពាក

appoint dtaing dtung តែងតាំង

appropriate (adj) som-rOOm សមរម្យ

April may-saa មេសា

area bor-ri-wayn បរិវេណ

argue jor-jairk ជជែក

arithmetic layk-kay-a-neut លេខគណិត

arm dai ដៃ

army gorng dtoa-up កងទ័ព

around *(around here)* nou jeut jeut nih នៅជិតៗនេះ

arrange jut jaing; ree-up jom ចាត់ចែង; រៀបចំ

arrest (v) jup ចាប់

arrive dol; moak/dtou dol ដល់; មក/ទៅដល់

art seu-la-bpa សិល្បៈ

artist seu-la-bpa-gor សិល្បករ

as for . . . jom-naik . . . weuñ; ai . . . weuñ ចំណែក . . . វិញ; ៨ . . . វិញ

as soon as plee-um ភ្លាម

ashamed k'maah ខ្មាស

ashtray jaan goo-ah ba-ray ចានគោះបារី

ask *(a question)* som soo-a សុំសួរ

  (for something) som សុំ

asleep dayk loo-uk ដេកលក់

assist joo-ay ជួយ

assistance jOOm-noo-ay ជំនួយ

assistant nay-uk jOOm-noo-ay អ្នកជំនួយ

association sa-maa-gOOm សមាគម

astrologer hao; kroo dtee-ay ហោរ; គ្រូទាយ

astrology hao-raa-saah ហោរាសាស្ត្រ

at nou នៅ

atmosphere bpa-ri-yaa-gaah បរិយាកាស

attach jorng p'joa-up ចងភ្ជាប់

audience *(listeners)* nay-uk s'dup អ្នកស្តាប់

August say-haa សីហា

aunt *(older sister of mother or father)* tom ធំ

(younger sister of mother or father) meeng មីង

Australia oa-straa-lee អូស្ត្រាលី

author nay-uk ni-bpoa-un អ្នកនិពន្ធ

authority om-naich អំណាច

automobile laan ឡាន

avoid jee-ah wee-ung ជៀសវាង

awake p'nyay-uk ភ្ញាក់

away *(absent)* meun nou មិននៅ

   go away! jeuñ dtou ចេញទៅ

ax bpoo-tao ពូថៅ

B

baby goan ngaa; goan ngait កូនង៉ា; កូនង៉ែត

bachelor gom-loh កម្លោះ

back *(of body)* k'norng ខ្នង

   at the back kaang grao-ee ខាងក្រោយ

bacteria buk-dtay-ree បាក់តេរី

bad aa-krok; koa-ich; meun la-or អាក្រក់; ខូច; មិនល្អ

   (food) pa-oam ផ្អម

   (fruit) ra-loo-ay រលួយ

bag tong ថង់

   paper bag tong gra-daah ថង់ក្រដាស

   handbag gra-boap yoo-a ក្របូបយួរ

bake *(in an oven)* dot ដុត

bald dtOOm-bpairk ទំពែក

ball bul បាល់

bamboo reu-say ឫស្សី

ban (n) *(prohibition)* bom-raam បំរាម

banana jayk ចេក

band *(music)* woo-ung playng វង់ភ្លេង

   (rubber) k'sai gao-soo ខ្សែកៅស៊ូ

bandage (n) bpong-seu-mong; rOOm-ra-boo-ah បង់សិម៉ង; រំប្អួស

bandit jao ចោរ

Bangkok baang-gork បាងកក

bank tor-nee-a-gee-a ធនាគារ

bar *(for drinking)* baa បារ

barbecue (v) ung; dot អាំង; ដុត

barbed wire loo-ah bon-laah លួសបន្លា

barber shop p'tay-ah gut sok ផ្ទះកាត់សក់

bargain (v) dtor t'lai តថ្លៃ

base *(military)* mool taan dtoa-up មូលដ្ឋានទ័ព

basket la-ay; goñ-jer ល្អី; កញ្ជើ

   (for moving earth) bong-gee បង្គី

bathe ngoot dteuk ងូតទឹក

bathroom bon-dtOOp dteuk បន្ទប់ទឹក

   (toilet) bong-goo-un បង្គន់

bathtub aang (ngoot)dteuk អាង(ងូត)ទឹក

Battambang but-dtom-bong ប្រាត់តំបង

battery t'mor ថ្ម

bay choong sa-mot ឈូងសមុទ្រ

be geu; jee-a គឺ; ជា

beach ch'nay sa-mot ឆ្នេរសមុទ្រ

bean son-daik សណ្ដែក

beard bpOOk jong-gaa ពុកចង្កា

beat (v) wee-ay វាយ

beautiful sa-aat; la-or ស្អាត; ល្អ
    (sound) bpi-roo-ah ពីរោះ

because bproo-ah; bpi-bproo-ah ព្រោះ; ពិព្រោះ

bed grair dayk គ្រែដេក

bedroom bon-tOOp dayk បន្ទប់ដេក

bee k'mOOm ឃ្មុំ

beef saich goa សាច់គោ

beer bee-yair បៀរ

before mOOn; bpee mOOn មុន; ពីមុន

beg som dtee-un សុំទាន

beggar nay-uk som dtee-un អ្នកសុំទាន

begin jup p'darm ចាប់ផ្ដើម

beginning pee-uk p'darm ភាគផ្ដើម

behind kaang grao-ee ខាងក្រោយ

believe jeu-a ជឿ

bell (large) joo-ung; ra-kay-ung ជួង; រគាំង
    (small) gon-deung; jong-grorng កណ្ដឹង; ចង្ក្រង

belong jee-a ra-boh ជារបស់

below kaang graom ខាងក្រោម

belt k'sai gra-wut ខ្សែក្រវាត់

bench jerng maa ជើងម៉ា

bend (v) bpoo-ut ពត់

best la-or jee-ung gay ល្អជាងគេ

bet (v) p'noa-ul ភ្នាល់

betray g'bot ក្បត់

better la-or jee-ung ល្អជាង

　I'm feeling better k'nyom kroa-un bar hai-ee ខ្ញុំគ្រាន់បើ
　ហើយ

between ra-wee-ung រវាង

beverage kreu-ung peuk គ្រឿងផឹក

bicycle gong; ra-dtayh gong កង់; រទេះកង់

big tom ធំ

bill som-bot សំបុត្រ

binoculars gai-o yeut កែវយឺត

biology jee-wee-a-saah ជីវសាស្ត្រ

bird buk-say បក្សី

birth gom-nart កំណើត

　give birth som-raal goan; ch'lorng dtoo-un-lay *(idiom.)*
　សំរាលកូន; ឆ្លងទន្លេ

birthday t'ngai gart ថ្ងៃកើត

bite (v) kum ខាំ

bitter *(taste)* l'weeng ល្វីង

black k'mao ខ្មៅ

blackboard g'daa kee-un ក្ដារខៀន

blame (v) bon-dtoah បន្ទោស

blanket poo-ay ភួយ

bleed jeuñ chee-um ចេញឈាម

blind (adj) kwuk ខ្វាក់

block (v) (obstruct) bpay-ung ពាំង

blood chee-um ឈាម

blow (wind) bok បក់

blue kee-o ខៀវ

   sky blue kee-o k'jay ខៀវខ្ចី

board (n) g'daa ក្ដារ

boast (v) oo-ut អួត

boat (ship) g'bul កប៉ាល់

   (small) dtook ទូក

body dtoo-a ខ្លួន

boil (v) dum ដាំ

   boiled water dteuk bpOOh ទឹកពុះ

bolt (n) ra-nOOk រនុក

bolt (v) duk ra-nOOk ដាក់រនុក

bone cha-eung ឆ្អឹង

book (n) see-a pou សៀវភៅ

book (v) bon-jee-a dtOOk បញ្ជាទុក

bookcase dtoo see-a pou ទូសៀវភៅ

border (frontier) bprOOm dain; jee-ay dain ព្រំដែន;

ជាយដែន

bored tOOñ dtroa-un ធុញទ្រាន់

born *(be born)* gart កើត

boss nay-uk dtroo-ut dtraa; jao fai អ្នកត្រួតត្រា; ចៅហ្វាយ

both dtay-ung bpee ទាំងពីរ

bother *(be a bother)* kwol; rOOm-kaan ខ្វល់; រំខាន

bottle dorp ដប

bottom *(body)* goot គូថ

   (of box) baat បាត

   (of hill) jerng ជើង

   (of page) jong ចុង

bowl *(soup)* jaan ចាន

box *(large)* heup ហិប

   (small) bpra-op ប្រអប់

box (v) dul ដាល់

boxer nay-uk bpra-dul អ្នកប្រដាល់

boxing gay-laa bpra-dul កីឡាប្រដាល់

boy bproh; k'mayng bproh ប្រុស; ក្មេងប្រុស

bracelet k'sai dai ខ្សែដៃ

brain koo-a g'baal ខួរក្បាល

brake (n) frung; bprung ប្រ៉ាង; ប្រាំង

brake (v) jup frung; jup bprung ចាប់ប្រ៉ាង; ចាប់ប្រាំង

branch *(office)* saa-kaa សាខា

   (tree) mairk មែក

brand *(trademark)* dtraa; yee hao ត្រា; យីហោ

brass   dtoo-ung daing   ទងដែង

brassiere   ao dtra-noa-up s'ray   អាវទ្រនាប់ស្រី

bread   nOOm-bpung   នំប៉័ង

break (v) *(something)*   baik   បែក

   (bones)   buk   បាក់

breakdown *(car)*   koa-ich   ខូច

breakfast   bai bpreuk   បាយព្រឹក

breath   dorng-harm   ដង្ហើម

breathe   dork dorng-harm   ដកដង្ហើម

bribe (n)   som-nook   សំណូក

bribe (v)   sook   សូក

brick   eut   ឥដ្ឋ

bridge   s'bpee-un   ស្ពាន

bright   pleu   ភ្លឺ

bring *(someone)*   noa-um . . . moak   នាំ ... មក

   (something)   yoak . . . moak   យក ... មក

broken   koa-ich   ខូច

broken-hearted   koa-ich jeut   ខូចចិត្ត

bronze   loo-ung-heun; som-reut   លងហិន; សំរិទ្ធ

broom   om-baoh   អំបោស

brother   *(elder)*   borng bproh   បងប្រុស ·

   (younger)   bpa-oan bproh   ប្អូនប្រុស

brother-in-law   *(elder)*   borng t'lai bproh   បងថ្លៃប្រុស

   (younger)   bpa-oan t'lai bproh   ប្អូនថ្លៃប្រុស

brothers and sisters   borng bpa-oan   បងប្អូន

brown bpoa-a t'naot ពណិត្នោត

brush (v) doh ដុស

bucket tung ថាំង

Buddha bpray-ah bpOOt ព្រះពុទ្ធ

Buddhism bpOOt-ta-saa-s'naa ពុទ្ធសាសនា

buffalo gra-bay ក្របី

build song; gor saang សង់; កសាង

building aa-gee-a អាគារ

bullet kroa-up gum-plerng គ្រាប់កាំភ្លើង

bump (v) joo-ul ជល់

bumpy (road) (plou) ra-lay-uk (ផ្លូវ)រលាក់

bureaucratism gaa-ri-yaa-lai-ni-yOOm ការិយាល័យនិយម

burglar jao ចោរ

Burma bpra-dtayh poo-mee-a ប្រទេសភូមា

burn (v) dot ដុត

bury gop កប់

bus laan ch'noo-ul ឡានឈ្នួល

bush gOOm-bpoat គុម្ពោត

business jOOm-noo-uñ ជំនួញ

   it's none of your business meun mairn geuch-gaa ra-boh
   nay-uk dtay មិនមែនកិច្ចការរបស់អ្នកទេ

businessman nay-uk jOOm-noo-uñ អ្នកជំនួញ

busy ra-woo-ul; k'mee-un dtOOm-nay រវល់; គ្មានទំនេរ

but dtai; bpon-dtai តែ; ប៉ុន្តែ

butter ber បឺរ

butterfly may om-bao មេអំបៅ
button lay-ew ឡេវ
buy dteuñ ទិញ
by dao-ee ដោយ

C

cabbage spay-ee k'daop ស្ពៃក្តោប
cabinet *(furniture)* dtoo ទូ
cable *(wire)* k'sai loo-ah ខ្សែលួស
cage dtrOOng ទ្រុង
cake nOOm នំ
calendar bra-gra-de-dtin ប្រក្រតិទិន
call *(shout)* s'raik ស្រែក
   to be called (something) hao ហៅ
   what's this called? nih hao taa ay? នេះហៅថាអ្វី?
Cambodia bpra-dtayh gum-bpOO-jee-a; s'rok k'mai
   ប្រទេសកម្ពុជា; ស្រុកខ្មែរ
Cambodian *(language)* pee-a-saa k'mai ភាសាខ្មែរ
   (person) k'mai ខ្មែរ
camera maa-seen tort roop ម៉ាស៊ីនថតរូប
camp *(army, refugee)* jOOm-rOOm ជំរំ
can *(v)* baan បាន
canal bpra-lai; bprairk jeek ប្រឡាយ; ព្រែកជីក
cancel lOOp jaol លុបចោល

cancer dom-bao ma-haa reek ដុំបៀមហារិក

candidate bpaik-ka-joon បេក្ខជូន

candle dtee-un ទៀន

cannot . . . . . . meun baan dtay . . .មិនបានទេ

capital *(money)* dtOOn; too-un ទុន; ធន

capital city *(kingdom)* ree-ich-tee-a-nee រាជធានី
   (republic) roa-ut-ta-tee-a-nee រដ្ឋធានី

captain *(army)* a-nOO-say-nee aik អនុសេនីឯក

capture jup ចាប់

car laan ឡាន

card *(playing)* bee-a បៀ
   business card nee-um bun នាមបណ្ណ

cardboard gra-daah gaa-dtong ក្រដាសការតុង

care for tai dtoa-um; tai ray-uk-saa ថែទាំ; ថែរក្សា

careful bpra-yut ប្រយ័ត្ន

careless t'wayh bpra-haih ធ្វេសប្រហែស

carpenter jee-ung cher ជាងឈើ

carry *(in the hands; light objects)* gun កាន់
   (in the hands; heavy objects) yoo-a យួរ
   (in the arms) bay; bpor បី; ពរ
   (on the back or shoulders) lee លី

cart ra-dtayh រទេះ

carton gra-daah gaa-dtong ក្រដាសការតុង

cash bpruk; loo-ee ប្រាក់; លុយ

cashier *(bank)* bay-laa-ti-gaa បេឡាធិការ

 (shop) nay-uk geut loo-ee អ្នកគិតលុយ

casket *(coffin)* k'daa m'chooh ក្តារម្ជួស

cat ch'maa ឆ្មា

catch (v) jup ចាប់

cauliflower p'gaa spay-ee ផ្កាស្ពៃ

cause (n) hait ហេតុ

cause (v) ao-ee; bon-daal ឲ្យ (អោយ);បណ្ដាល

cave roong រូង

cease-fire gaa chOOp buñ ការឈប់បាញ់

ceiling bpi-daan ពិតាន

cement see-mong ស៊ីម៉ង

cemetery dtee bpaa-chaa ទីប៉ាឆា

center gon-daal កណ្ដាល

centimeter song-dti-mait សង់ទីម៉ែត្រ

ceremony bpi-tee ពិធី

certain jee-a bpraa-got ជាប្រាកដ

certainly *(of course)* bpraa-got mairn hai-ee; neung hai-ee
 ប្រាកដមែនហើយ;ហ្នឹងហើយ

certificate som-bot សំបុត្រ

chain j'ra-wuk ច្រវាក់

chair gao-ay កៅអី

Cham jaam ចាម

chance ao-gaah ឱកាស

change (n) gaa bprai bproo-ul ការប្រែប្រួល

 (v) plah b'doa ផ្លាស់ប្ដូរ

change one's mind   plah gOOm-neut; plah jeut
ផ្លាស់គំនិត; ផ្លាស់ចិត្ត

charcoal   t'yoong   ធ្យូង

charge (v)   geut t'lai   គិតថ្លៃ

chase (after)   dayñ dtaam   ដេញតាម

chase (away)   dayñ jeuñ   ដេញចេញ

chat (v)   ni-yee-ay layng   និយាយលេង

cheap   taok   ថោក

cheat (v)   baok; loo-ich bon-lom   ប្រោក; លួចបន្លំ

check (n) (money)   saik; chaik   សែក; ឆែក

check (v)   chaik; chaik-chay   ឆែក; ឆែកឆេរ
   chaik merl   ឆែកមើល

chemistry (chemical)   kee-mee   គីមី
   chemical weapons   aa-wOOt kee-mee   អាវុធគីមី

chest (body)   ok   អុក

chew   dtOOm-bpee-a   ទំពារ

chicken   moa-un   មាន់

chief   may   មេ

child (one's own)   goan   កូន

child, children (in general)   k'mayng   ក្មេង

chilli   m'tayh   ម្ទេស

chin   jong-gaa   ចង្កា

China   bpra-dtayh jeun   ប្រទេសចិន

Chinese (adj)   jeun   ចិន

Chinese (language)   pee-a-saa jeun   ភាសាចិន

(person) jeun ចិន

chisel bpoo-un-lee-uk ពន្លាក

choice gaa j'rerh rerh ការជ្រើសរើស

choke j'ra-baich gor ច្របាចក

cholera aa-son-na-roak; jOOm-ngeu joh ga-oo-ut
អាសន្នរោគ; ជម្ងឺចុះក្អួត

choose rerh រើស

chopsticks jong-geuh ចង្កឹះ

Christ bpray-ah yay-soo ព្រះយេស៊ូ

Christianity kreuh saa-s'naa គ្រិស្តសាសនា

Christmas bon noa-ail បុណ្យណូអែល

church wi-hee-a វិហារ

cigarette ba-ray ប៉ារី

cinema roang gon; roang pee-up-yoo-un រោងកុន;
រោងភាពយន្ត

circle woo-ung mool វង់មូល

circuit *(electric)* plou uk-kee-sa-nee ផ្លូវអគ្គីសនី

city dtee grong ទីក្រុង

civil servant nay-uk ree-ich-a-gaa; nay-uk roa-ut-ta-gaa
អ្នករាជការ; អ្នករដ្ឋការ

civilian see-weul ស៊ីវិល

clap (hands) dtay-ah dai ទះដៃ

class t'nuk ថ្នាក់

   first class t'nuk dtee moo-ay ថ្នាក់ទីមួយ

   second class t'nuk dtee bpee ថ្នាក់ទីពីរ

class (*social*) wun-nah វណ្ណៈ

   capitalist class wun-nah nee-ay dtOOn វណ្ណនាយទុន

classroom bon-dtOOp ree-un បន្ទប់រៀន

clause (*in a contract*) kor ១

clean (*to be clean*) sa-aat; j'ray-ah ស្អាត; ជ្រេះ

   to make clean som-aat; jOOm-ray-ah; សំអាត; ជំរះ

   doh-lee-ung ដុសលាង

clear ch'bah ច្បាស់

   you speak Khmer clearly ni-yee-ay k'mai ch'bah

   និយាយខ្មែរច្បាស់

clever ch'laat; bpraach-n'yaa ឆ្លាត; ប្រាជ្ញា

climate aa-gaah-sa-tee-ut អាកាសធាតុ

climb larng ឡើង

clock nee-a-li-gaa នាឡិកា

close (*near*) jeut; k'bai ជិត; កៀរ

close (*shut*) beut បិទ

cloth som-bpoo-ut សំពត់

clothes kao-ao ខោអាវ; som-lee-uk bom-bpay-uk

   សំលៀកបំពាក់

   clothes hanger bpra-dup bp'yoo-a kao-ao ប្រដាប់ព្យួរ

   ខោអាវ

cloud bpor-bpork ពពក

coast ch'nay; ch'nay sa-mot ឆ្នេរ; ឆ្នេរសមុទ្រ

coat ao tom អាវធំ

cobra bpoo-ah bpor-bplay-uk ពស់ពញ្ញាក់

cockroach gon-laat កន្លាត

coconut doang ដូង

coffee gaa-fay កាហ្វេ

coffin g'dah m'chooh ក្តារម្ចូស

coins *(small change)* loo-ee ree-ay; bpruk guk លុយរាយ; ប្រាក់កាក់

cola goa-laa កូឡា

cold (adj) ra-ngee-a; dtra-jay-uk រងា; ត្រជាក់

  I feel cold k'nyom ra-ngee-a ខ្ញុំរងា

cold (n) krOOn p'daah sai គ្រុនផ្តាសសាយ

  I have a cold k'nyom krOOn p'daah sai
ខ្ញុំគ្រុនផ្តាសសាយ

collar gor ao កអាវ

collect bpra-mool ប្រមូល

college ma-haa-wit-yee-a-lai មហាទិព្យាល័យ

collide bok បុក

collision *(car collision)* laan bok k'nee-a ឡានបុកគ្នា

color bpoa-a ពណ៌

comb (n) graah ក្រាស

comb (v) (hair) seut (sok) សិត(សក់)

come moak មក

  come here! moak ai nih មកឯនេះ

  come in joal moak ចូលមក

  where do you come from? loak moak bpee naa?
លោកមកពីណា?

comedy   reu-ung gom-bplaing   រឿងកំប្លែង

comfortable   s'roo-ul   ស្រួល

communism   kom-mew-nih ni-yOOm   កុម្មុយនិស្តនិយម

communist(s)   (bpoo-uk) kom-mew-nih   (ពួក)កុម្មុយនិស្ត

communist party   bpuk kom-mew-nih   បក្សកុម្មុយនិស្ត

company *(business)*   grom hOOn; bor-ri-sut   ក្រុមហ៊ុន;
បរិស័ទ

compare   bpree-up tee-up   ប្រៀបធៀប

complain   bp'deung; dtor waa   ប្ដឹង; តវ៉ា

concerning   om-bpee; jom-bpoo-ah   អំពី; ចំពោះ

concrete *(cement)*   see-mong bay-dtong   ស៊ីម៉ង់បេតុង

condition (of health)   layk-ka-na (sok-ka-pee-up)   លក្ខណៈ(សុខភាព)

condom   s'raom un-naa-mai   ស្រោមអនាម័យ

confidence   saych-ga-day dtOOk jeut   សេចក្ដីទុកចិត្ត

confused   lop; j'ra-lom   ឡប់; ច្រឡំ

connect   p'joa-up   ភ្ជាប់

consonant   bp'yuñ-jay-a-nay-uk   ព្យញ្ជនៈ

constantly   ot chOOp chor   ឥតឈប់ឈរ

constitution   roa-ut-ta-toa-a-ma-nOOñ   រដ្ឋធម្មនុញ្ញ

construct   sorng; gor saang   សង់; កសាង

consul   gong-sOOl   កុងស៊ុល

consulate   s'taan gong-sOOl   ស្ថានកុងស៊ុល

consult   bpi-kroo-ah; som yoa-bol   ពិគ្រោះ; សុំយោបល់

consultant   dtee bpreuk-saa   ទីប្រឹក្សា

consumer goods   kreu-ung op-bpa-poak   គ្រឿងឧបភោគ

contact *(get in touch with)*   dtay-uk-dtorng   ទាក់ទង

contented *(happy)*   sop-bai jeut; s'roo-ul jeut; bpeuñ jeut
សប្បាយចិត្ត; ស្រួលចិត្ត; ពេញចិត្ត

continue   dtor; bon-dtor   ត; បន្ត

contract (n)   geuch son-yaa; gong-dtraa   កិច្ចសន្យា;កុងត្រា
   break a contract   l'merh geuch son-yaa   លើ្មសកិច្ចសន្យា
   sign a contract   joh hut-ta-layk-kaa ler geuch son-yaa
ចុះហត្ថលេខាលើកិច្ចសន្យា

control (v)   gun gup   កាន់កាប់
   under the control of   graom gaa gun gup
ក្រោមការកាន់កាប់

convenient   s'roo-ul; som-goo-a   ស្រួល; សមគួរ

cook (n)   nay-uk dum slor   អ្នកដាំស្ល

cook (v)   dum slor; t'wer bai   ដាំស្ល; ធ្វើបាយ

cookie   nOOm dot   នំដុត

cool *(to be cool)*   dtra-jay-uk   ត្រជាក់
   to cool something   t'wer . . . ao-ee dtra-jay-uk
ធ្វើ . . . ឱ្យត្រជាក់

cooperate   roo-um gom-lung   រួមកម្លាំង

copier *(machine)*   kreu-ung tort jom-lorng   គ្រឿងថតចម្លង

copper   s'bpoa-un   ស្ពាន់

copy (n)   ch'bup jom-lorng   ច្បាប់ចម្លង
   (v)   jom-lorng   ចម្លង

cork *(stopper)*   ch'nok   ឆ្នុក

corn bpoat ពោត

corner j'rOOng ជ្រុង

   corner of a room gee-un bon-dtOOp កៀនបន្ទប់

   street corner j'rOOng plou ជ្រុងផ្លូវ

correct dtrou ត្រូវ

cost dom-lai; t'lai តម្លៃ; ថ្លៃ

cotton wool som-lay សំឡី

cough ga-ork ក្អក

count roa-up រាប់

country (*nation*) bpra-dtayh; s'rok ប្រទេស; ស្រុក

countryside s'rok s'rai ស្រុកស្រែ

coup d'état roa-ut-ta-bpra-haa រដ្ឋប្រហារ

course (*study*) mOOk wi-jee-a មុខវិជ្ជា

   of course neung hai-ee ហ្នឹងហើយ

court (*law*) saa-laa gut g'day សាលាកាត់ក្ដី

cousin bporng-bpa-oan ji-doan moo-ay បងប្អូនជីដូនមួយ

cow goa គោ

crab g'daam ក្ដាម

crawl loon លូន

crazy (*foolish*) ch'goo-ut ឆ្កួត

cremate dot sop ដុតសព

cremation gaa boo-jee-a sop ការបូជាសព

cricket (*insect*) jong-reut ចង្រិត

crime bot-o-greut បទឧក្រិដ្ឋ

commit a crime   bpra-bpreut bot-o-greut

ប្រព្រឹត្តបទឧក្រិដ្ឋ

criminal   nay-uk dtoah; o-greut-ta-gor   អ្នកទោស;
ឧក្រិដ្ឋករ

crippled   bpi-gaa   ពិការ

criticize   dti-dtee-un   ទិទៀន

crocodile   gra-bper   ក្រពើ

crops   dom-num   ដំណាំ

cross (v)   ch'lorng gut   ឆ្លងកាត់

cross a street   ch'lorng plou   ឆ្លងផ្លូវ

crossroads   plou gaing   ផ្លូវកែង

crowded   jong-ee-ut   ចង្អៀត

cruel   koa-kou   យោរយៅ

cry *(shout)*   s'raik   ស្រែក

   (tears)   yOOm   យំ

cucumber   dtror-sok   ត្រសក់

culture   wup-pa-toa-a   វប្បធម៌

cup   bpairng   ពែង

cupboard   dtoo   ទូ

curfew   bom-raam goa-jor   បំរាមគោចរ

curry   gaa-ree   ការី

curtain   ra-nay-ung   រនាំង

custom   dtOOm-nee-um dtOOm-loa-up;   ទំនៀមទម្លាប់;
   bpra-bpay-nee   ប្រពៃណី

customs department gra-soo-ung goy ក្រសួងគយ

cut gut កាត់

cyclo see-kloa ស៊ីក្លូ

D

dam *(dike)* dtOOm-nOOp ទំនប់

dance (n) ra-bum របាំ

dance (v) roa-um រាំ

danger kroo-ah t'nuk; on-dta-rai គ្រោះថ្នាក់; អន្តរាយ

dangerous mee-un kroo-ah t'nu k មានគ្រោះថ្នាក់

Dangrek Mountains p'nOOm dorng-rairk ភ្នំដងរែក

dare (to) hee-un ហ៊ាន

date *(what date . . . ?)* . . . t'ngai dtee bpon-maan?
. . . ថ្ងៃទីប៉ុន្មាន?

daughter goan s'ray កូនស្រី

dawn bpra-leum ព្រលឹម

day t'ngai ថ្ងៃ

   day after tomorrow kaan s'aik ខានស្អែក

   day before yesterday m'seul m'ngai ម្សិលម្ងៃ

   day off t'ngai chOOp ថ្ងៃឈប់

dead s'lup ស្លាប់

deaf t'long ថ្លង់

debt bom-nol បំណុល

December t'noo ធ្នូ

decide　som-raich jeut; dtung jeut　សំរេចចិត្ត; តាំងចិត្ត

declare　jaing; bpra-gaah; t'laing　ចែង; ប្រកាស; ថ្លែង

deep　j'rou　ជ្រៅ

defeat (v)　ch'nay-ah　ឈ្នះ
　　(be) defeated　juñ　ចាញ់

defend　gaa bpee-a　ការពារ

degree (temperature)　ong-saa　អង្សា
　　(university)　suñ-n'yaa-but　សញ្ញាប័ត្រ

deliberately　dao-ee jay-dta-naa　ដោយចេតនា

delicious　ch'nguñ　ឆ្ងាញ់

delighted　dtrayk-or　ត្រេកអរ

democracy　bpra-jee-a-teup-bpa-dtay　ប្រជាធិបតេយ្យ

dengue fever　grOOn chee-um　គ្រុនឈាម

dentist　bpairt t'meuñ　ពេទ្យធ្មេញ

deny　bpa-de-sayt　បដិសេធ

depart　jeuñ　ចេញ

department (govt.)　grom　ក្រុម

depend: it depends on . . .　s'raich dtai . . .　ស្រេចតែ . . .

deposit (v) (money)　gork bpruk　កក់ប្រាក់

descend　joh　ចុះ

design (n)　k'baich　ក្បាច់

desk　dto　តុ

dessert　bong-aim　បង្អែម

destroy　gom-dtaych　កំទេច

detour　plou wee-ung　ផ្លូវវាង

develop *(a country)* t'wer ao-ee loot loa-ah
ធ្វើឱ្យលូតលាស់

(film) lee-ung (feem) លាង (ហ្វីម)

development gaa jom-rarn loot loa-ah; up-pi-woat-tay-a-na-
pee-up ការចំរើនលូតលាស់; អភិវឌ្ឍនភាព

dialect kree-um pee-a-saa គ្រាមភាសា

diamond bpeuch ពេជ្រ

diarrhea roak joh ree-uk រោគចុះរាក

dictatorship ra-borp p'daich-gaa របបផ្ដាច់ការ

dictionary wuch-a-naa-nOO-grom វចនានុក្រម

die s'lup ស្លាប់

different koh; bplaik ខុស; ថ្លែក

difficult bpi-baak; lOOm-baak ពិបាក; លំបាក

dig jeek ជីក

dining room bon-dtOOp n'yum bai បន្ទប់ញ៉ាំបាយ

diploma suñ-n'yaa-but សញ្ញាបត្រ

diplomacy gaa dtoot ការទូត

diplomat dtoot ទូត

direct *(adj)* dtrong ត្រង់

direction *(north)* dtih (kaang jerng) ទិស (ខាងជើង)

director ut-ti-gaa; jaang waang អធិការ; ចាងហ្វាង

dirty gror-kwok កខ្វក់

disabled bpi-gaa ពិការ

disappear but បាត់

disarmament gaa dtOOm-lay-uk aa-wOOt

ការទម្លាក់អាវុធ

discuss *(about)* bpi-kroo-ah om-bpee ពិគ្រោះអំពី
   (together) jor-jairk k'nee-a; ជជែកគ្នា

disease roak; jOOm-ngeu រោគ; ជម្ងឺ
   contagious disease jOOm-ngeu ch'lorng ជម្ងឺឆ្លង

dish jaan ចាន

dishonest dtOOch-ja-reut ទុច្ចរិត

dismiss deuñ jeuñ ដេញចេញ

dissolve rOOm-lee-ay រំលាយ

distance jom-ngai ចម្ងាយ

distilled water dteuk beut ទឹកបិត

distillery roang t'wer s'raa រោងធ្វើស្រា

district s'rok ស្រុក

ditch (n) s'naam ploo-ah ស្នាមភ្លោះ

dive (v) mOOch មុច

divide jairk ចែក

division *(within govt. department)* p'naik ផ្នែក

divorce (v) lairng lay-ah k'nee-a លែងលះគ្នា

dizzy weul mOOk វិលមុខ

do t'wer ធ្វើ

doctor bpairt; kroo bpairt ពេទ្យ; គ្រូពេទ្យ

document (n) aik-ga-saa ឯកសារ

dog ch'gai ឆ្កែ

doll goan gra-mom កូនក្រមុំ

dollar dol-laa ដុល្លា

don't gom ... (ay) កុំ ... (ទេ)

don't mention it meun ay dtay មិនអ្វីទេ

door twee-a ទ្វារ

double goo គូ

double room bon-dtOOp som-rup bpee nay-uk
បន្ទប់សំរាប់ពីរនាក់

doubt (v) song-sai សង្ស័យ

down joh ចុះ

downstairs kaang graom· ខាងក្រោម

dozen loa ឡូ

drama *(play)* lã-kaon ល្ខោន

draw (a picture) goo (roop) គូ(រូប)

drawer (of cabinet) tort (dtoo) ថត(ទូ)

dream (v) yoo-ul sop យល់សប្ត

dress (n) som-lee-uk bom-bpay-uk សម្លៀកបំពាក់

   (v) s'lee-uk bpay-uk ស្លៀកពាក់

dried and salted ngee-ut ងៀត

drink (v) peuk ផឹក

drive (a vehicle) bark (laan) បើក(ឡាន)

driver nay-uk bark laan អ្នកបើកឡាន

drop (v) t'lay-uk ធ្លាក់

drown loo-ung dteuk លង់ទឹក

drug *(medicine)* t'num ថ្នាំ

   (narcotics) k'reu-ung n'yee-un គ្រឿងញៀន

drugstore *(pharmacy)* haang loo-uk t'num; ហាងលក់ថ្នាំ;

ao-sot s'taan ឱ្យសថ្ថាន

drum s'gor ស្គរ

drunk s'ra-weung ស្រវឹង

dry *(clothes)* s'ngoo-ut ស្ងួត

   (weather) ray-ung រាំង

dry clean lee-ung s'ngoo-ut លាងស្ងួត

duck dtee-a ទា

dull reul រិល

dump (v) juk jaol ចាក់ចោល

durian too-reen ធុរេន

during ra-wee-ung រវាង

duty gaa ngee-a ការងារ

dwell nou; roo-ah nou នៅ; រស់នៅ

dysentery (jOOm-ngeu) moo-ul; rohk ree-uk moo-ul
   (ជម្ងឺ)មូល; រោគរាគមូល

E

each ni-moo-ay និមួយ

ear dtra-jee-uk ត្រចៀក

early *(before expected)* mOOn maong មុនម៉ោង

   (morning) bpreuk ព្រឹក

   early morning bpra-leum ព្រលឹម

   get up early graok bpee bpra-leum ក្រោកពីព្រលឹម

earn a living   rork see   រកស៊ី

earring   gra-ẉeul   ក្រវិល

earth *(soil)*   day   ដី

east   gart; kaang gart   កើត; ខាងកើត

easy   s'roo-ul; ngee-ay   ស្រួល; ងាយ

eat *(colloquial)* n'yum   ញ៉ាំ

   (formal) dtor-dtoo-ul dtee-un   ទទួលទាន

   (polite) bpi-saa   ពិសា

   (rural) hoap   ហូប

   (vulgar) see   ស៊ី

economics   sayt-ta-saah   សេដ្ឋសាស្ត្រ

economy   sayt-ta-geuch   សេដ្ឋកិច្ច

edge   gairm   គែម

education   gaa seuk-saa   ការសិក្សា

effect (n)   pol   ផល

efficiency   bpra-seut-ti-pee-up   ប្រសិទ្ធិភាព

egg   bporng   ពង

eight   bprum bay   ប្រាំបី

eighty   bpait seup   ប៉ែតសិប

either *(either X or Y)*   X gor baan Y gor baan   X ក៏បាន Y ក៏បាន

   either one will do   moo-ay naa gor baan   មួយណាក៏បាន

elect   boh ch'naot; j'rerh dtung   បោះឆ្នោត; ជ្រើសតាំង

election   gaa boh ch'naot   ការបោះឆ្នោត

   general election   gaa boh ch'naot sa-gorl   ការបោះ

ឆ្នោតសកល

electrician jee-ung plerng; jee-ung uk-gee-sa-nee ជាង
ភ្លើង; ជាងអគ្គីសនី

electricity uk-gee-sa-nee អគ្គីសនី

elephant dom-ray ដំរី

elevator joo-un-dar yoang ជណ្ដើរយោង

eleven *(colloquial)* moo-ay don-dop មួយដណ្ដប់
    (formal) dop moo-ay ដប់មួយ

embarrassed dterh dtoa-ul; ee-un kloo-un ទើសទាល់;
អៀនខ្លួន

embassy s'taan dtoot ស្ថានទូត

emergency *(in an emergency)* kree-a aa-son គ្រាអាសន្ន

employ joo-ul ជួល

employee ni-yoa-jeut និយោជិត

employer ni-yoa-joo-uk និយោជក

employment gaa ngee-a ការងារ

empty dtor-dtay; dtOOm-nay ទទេ; ទំនេ

end jong ចុង
    in the end nou dtee bom-pot នៅទីបំផុត

endure too-un; ot too-un ធន់; អត់ធន់

enemy sa-dtrou; k'mung សត្រូវ; ខ្មាំង

energy gom-lung កម្លាំង

engaged *(to be married)* baan p'joa-up bpee-uk hai-ee
 បានភ្ជាប់ពាក្យហើយ

engine kreu-ung yoo-un គ្រឿងយន្ត

engineer wi-s'wa-gor វិស្វករ

engineering wi-s'wa-gum វិស្វកម្ម

England bpra-dtayh ong-klayh ប្រទេសអង់គ្លេស

English (adj) ong-klayh អង់គ្លេស

English *(language)* pee-a-saa ong-klayh ភាសាអង់គ្លេស

  (person) ong-klayh អង់គ្លេស

enjoy sop-bai សប្បាយ

enough krOOp kroa-un; l'morm គ្រប់គ្រាន់; ល្មម

  that's enough l'morm hai-ee ល្មមហើយ

enter joal ចូល

  enter the monkhood boo-ah បួស

entrance twee-a joal ទ្វារចូល

envelope s'raom som-bot ស្រោមសំបុត្រ

equal (to) s'mar (neung) ស្មើ (នឹង)

equipment kreu-ung bpra-dup គ្រឿងប្រដាប់

era sa-mai សម័យ

erase lOOp លុប

eraser jor lOOp ជ័រលុប

escape (v) loo-ich roo-ut jeuñ លួចរត់ចេញ

especially jee-a bpi-sayh ជាពិសេស

establish bark; dtung; bong-gart បើក; តាំង; បង្កើត

Europe eu-rop អឺរ៉ុប

evening l'ngee-ich ល្ងាច

  early evening bpra-lOOp ព្រលប់

event hait-gaa ហេតុការណ៍

ever *(to have ever done something)* dail ដែល

every roa-ul រាល់

everyone dtay-ung oh k'nee-a ទាំងអស់គ្នា

everything a-way a-way dtay-ung oh អ្វី ៗ ទាំងអស់

everywhere krOOp dtee gon-laing គ្រប់ទីកន្លែង

exact goo-ut; dtrou តត់; ត្រូវ

exam *(take an exam)* bra-long ប្រឡង

examine bpi-neut ពិនិត្យ

example gOOm-roo; dtoo-a yaang គំរូ; គួយ៉ាង

exceed j'rOOl ជ្រុល

except (for) lerk lairng dtai លើកលែងតែ

exchange (v) *(money)* b'doa (bpruk) ប្តូរប្រាក់

   exchange X for Y doa X jee-a Y ដូរ X ជា Y

excuse (v) soam dtoah សូមទោស

   excuse me soam dtoah សូមទោស

execute *(a criminal)* bpra-haa jee-weut ប្រហារជីវិត

exercise (v) *(physical)* hut bpraan ហាត់ប្រាន

exhausted *(tired)* oh gom-lung អស់កម្លាំង

   (used up) oh អស់

expect song-keum សង្ឃឹម

expel bon-dayñ jaol បណ្ដេញចោល

expenses jom-nai ចំណាយ

expensive t'lai ថ្លៃ

experience bot bpi-saot បទពិសោធន៍

experiment (v) *(test)* bpi-saot ពិសោធន៍

---

expert (n)   nay-uk jOOm-nee-uñ gaa   អ្នកជំនាញការ

explain   bpoo-un-yoo-ul   ពន្យល់

explode   p'dtOOh   ផ្ទុះ

explosion   bon-dtOOh; gaa p'dtOOh   បន្ទុះ; ការផ្ទុះ

export   noa-um jeuñ   នាំចេញ

extension   gaa bon-dtor   ការបន្ត

extinguish   rOOm-loo-ut   រំលត់

extinguisher *(fire)*   kreu-ung rOOm-loo-ut plerng
 គ្រឿងរំលត់ភ្លើង

extremely   bpayk   ពេក

extremist(s)   bpoo-uk j'rOOl ni-yOOm   ពួកជ្រុលនិយម

eye   p'nairk   ភ្នែក

eyebrow   jeuñ-jarm   ចិញ្ចើម

eyelash   roam p'nairk   រោមភ្នែក

F

face (n)   mOOk   មុខ

   lose face   up mOOk   អាប់មុខ

   save face   meun ao-ee buk mOOk   មិនឱ្យប្រាក់មុខ

fact   gaa bpeut   ការពិត

   i. fact   dtaam (gaa) bpeut   តាម(ការ)ពិត

factory   roang juk   រោងចក្រ

fail (an exam)   (bpra-lorng) t'lay-uk   (ប្រឡង) ធ្លាក់

fair *(festival)*   bon   បុណ្យ

   (just)   dtreum dtrou; goo-a sorm   ត្រឹមត្រូវ; គួរសម

fall asleep   dayk loo-uk   ដេកលក់

fall over   doo-ul   ដួល

false *(fake)*   glaing   ក្លែង

   (untrue)   meun bpeut   មិនពិត

family   kroo-a-saa   គ្រួសារ

famine   gaa ot bai   ការអត់បាយ

famous   l'bay; l'bay l'baañ   ល្បី; ល្បីល្បាញ

fan (n)   pleut   ផ្លិត

   (electric)   dong-hul (uk-gee-sa-nee)   ដង្ហាល់(អគ្គីសនី)

far   ch'ngai   ឆ្ងាយ

fare   t'lai ch'noo-ul   ថ្លៃឈ្នួល

farmer   nay-uk s'rai; gu-si-gor   អ្នកស្រែ; កសិករ

   (rice) farming   t'wer s'rai   ធ្វើស្រែ

fashion   moad   ម៉ូដ

fashionable   moad dtOOm-ꞑerp   ម៉ូដទំនើប

fast   leu-un; chup   លឿន; ឆាប់

fat (adj)   toa-ut   ធាត់

fat (n)   k'luñ   ខ្លាញ់

fate   wee-a-sa-naa   វាសនា

father   oa-bpOOk   ឪពុក

father-in-law   oa-bpOOk k'mayk   ឪពុកក្មេក

fault   gom-hoh   កំហុស

fear (n)   saych g'day k'laich   សេចក្ដីខ្លាច

fear (v) k'laich ខ្លាច

February gom-pay-a កុម្ភៈ

fee t'lai ថ្លៃ

female s'ray ស្រី

fence ra-borng របង

fertilizer jee ជី

festival bpi-dtee bon ពិធីបុណ្យ

fever jOOm-ngeu grOOn g'dao ជម្ងឺក្រុនក្តៅ

few dteuch តិច

field (rice field) s'rai ស្រែ

   sports field t'lee-a gay-laa ឆ្នាកីឡា

fifteen dop bprum; bprum don-dop ដប់ប្រាំ; ប្រាំដណ្ដប់

fight (v) (brawl) wee-ay dtop វាយតប់

   (for justice) dtor soo តស៊ូ

   (soldier) bpra-yOOt ប្រយុទ្ធ

fill bom-bpeuñ បំពេញ

film (movie) gon; pee-up-yoo-un កុន; ភាពយន្ត

   (for camera) feem tort roop ហ្វីមថតរូប

finally nou dtee bom-pot នៅទីបំផុត

find rork kerñ រកឃើញ

   I can't find it k'nyom rork bpOOm kerñ ខ្ញុំរកពុំឃើញ

fine (n) bpruk bpi-nay ប្រាក់ពិន័យ

finger m'ree-um dai ម្រាមដៃ

finish (something) boñ-jop; bong-hai-ee បញ្ចប់; បង្ហើយ

finished jop ចប់

fire (n) plerng cheh ភ្លើងឆេះ

fire (v) *(a gun)* buñ បាញ់

  (dismiss) bon-dayñ jeuñ bpee gaa ngee-a

បណ្ដេញចេញពីការងារ

firm (n) *(company)* grom hOOn ក្រុមហ៊ុន

first dtee moo-ay ទីមួយ

  first of all mOOn dom-boang មុនដំបូង

fish (n) dt'ray ត្រី

fish (v) *(with line)* s'dtooch dt'ray ស្ទូចត្រី

  (with net) bong dt'ray បង់ត្រី

fish sauce dteuk dt'ray ទឹកត្រី

fisherman nay-uk nay-saat dt'ray អ្នកនេសាទត្រី

fit (clothes) sorm សម

five bprum ប្រាំ

fix (v) *(repair)* joo-ah jOOl ជួសជុល

  (e.g., price) gom-not កំណត់

flag dtoo-ung ទង់

flat (adj) ree-up s'mar រៀបស្មើ

  (apartment) p'dtay-ah l'wairng ផ្ទះល្វែង

flea(s) jai ch'gai ចៃឆ្កែ

flee roo-ut jeuñ; pee-ah រត់ចេញ; ភៀស

float (v) on-dait អណ្ដែត

flood dteuk joo-un ទឹកជន់

floor g'daa graal ក្ដារក្រាល

  (story) joa-un ជាន់

flour m'sao mee ម្សៅមី

flow (v) hoa ហូរ

flower (n) p'gaa ផ្កា

fly (n) *(insect)* roo-ee រុយ

   (v) hoh ហោះ

fold bot បត់

follow dtaam តាម

food *(rice)* bai; m'hoap បាយ; ម្ហូប

foolish pler; l'ngoo-ung ភ្លើ; ល្ងង់

foot jerng ជើង

football fOOt-bul ហ្វុតបัល

  play football dtoa-ut bul ទាត់បាល់

for som-rup សម្រាប់

  (in order to) darm-bay (neung) ដើម្បី (និង)

forbid haam ហាម

force (n) gom-lung កម្លាំង

force (v) bong-kom បង្ខំ

foreign bor-ra-dtayh បរទេស

foreigner joo-un bor-ra-dtayh ជនបរទេស

forest bpray-ee ព្រៃ

forget pleuch ភ្លេច

forgive a-pay dtoah; ot dtoah អភัយទោស; អត់ទោស

fork sorm សម

formal plou-gaa ផ្លូវការ

former mOOn មុន

formerly bpee mOOn ពីមុន

fortune teller kroo dtee-ay គ្រូទាយ

four boo-un បួន

fragile s'roo-ay; ngee-ay baik ស្រួយ; ងាយបែក

    Fragile: Handle with Care ngee-ay baik:joa bpra-yut

    ងាយបែក - ចូរប្រយ័ត្ន

France bpra-dtayh baa-rung ប្រទេសបារាំង

free *(no charge)* ot bong t'lai ឥតបង់ថ្លៃ

    free time dtOOm-nay ទំនេរ

freedom say-ray-pee-up សេរីភាព

French *(language)* pee-a-saa baa-rung ភាសាបារាំង

frequently n'yeuk-n'yoa-up ញឹកញ្យាប់

fresh s'roh ស្រស់

    fresh water dteuk saap ទឹកសាប

Friday t'ngai sok ថ្ងៃសុក្រ

fried rice bai chaa បាយឆា

friend bpoo-uk maak; meut ពួកម៉ាក; មិត្ត

friendship may-dtray-pee-up; mit-dta-pee-up មេត្រីភាព; មិត្តភាព

frighten bom-pay; gom-laich បំភ័យ; កំឡ្យាច

frightened klaich ខ្លាច

frog gong-gaip; ong-gaip កង្កែប; អង្កែប

from bpee ពី

front mOOk មុខ

    in front of nou kaang mOOk នៅខាងមុខ

frozen gork កក

fruit plai cher ផ្លែឈើរ

fry jee-un ចៀន

   deep fry bom-bporng បំពង

   stir fry chaa ឆា

full bpeuñ ពេញ

   (from eating) cha-ait ឆ្អែត

fun *(to have fun)* layng sop-bai លេងសប្បាយ

funeral bon k'maoch បុណ្យខ្មោច

funny gom-bplaing កំប្លែង

furniture kreu-ung dto dtoo គ្រឿងតុទូ.

future a-naa-goo-ut អនាគត

G

gamble layng l'baing see-sorng លេងល្បែងស៊ីសង

game l'baing ល្បែង

garage *(at house)* roang jort laan រោងចតឡ្លាន

   (for repairs) gon-laing joo-ah jOOl កន្លែងជួសជុល

garbage som-raam សំរាម

garden soo-un; soo-un ch'baa ស្ងន; ស្ងនច្បារ

gardener nay-uk tai soo-un ch'baa អ្នកថែស្ងនច្បារ

garlic k'dteum sor ខ្ទឹមស

gasoline bprayng sung; sung ប្រេងសាំង; សាំង

gate t'wee-a ទ្វារ

gather *(collect)* bpra-moal; bpra-moal p'dOOm ប្រមូល; ប្រមូលផ្ដុំ

gem t'boang ត្បូង

general *(in general)* jee-a dtoo dtou ជាទូទៅ

generous jeut sop-bo-roh ចិត្តសប្បុរស

gentle s'loat ស្លូត

gentleman so-pee-up bo-roh សុភាពបុរស

genuine mairn dtairn មែនទែន

geography poo-mi-saah ភូមិសាស្ត្រ

germ may-roak មេរោគ

German aa-leu-mong អាឡឺម៉ង់

Germany bpra-dtayh aa-leu-mong ប្រទេសអាឡឺម៉ង់

get baan បាន

get off *(a train)* joh ចុះ

get on *(a train)* larng ឡើង

ghost k'maoch ខ្មោច

gift jOOm-noon ជំនូន

ginger k'nyay ខ្ញី

girl k'mayng s'ray ក្មេងស្រី

give ao-ee ឲ្យ (អោយ)

give birth to som-raal goan សំរាលកូន

glad sop-bai; dtrayk-or សប្បាយ; ត្រេកអរ

glass (n) gai-o កែវ

glasses *(spectacles)* wain dtaa វែនតា

sunglasses wain dtaa k'mao វ៉ែនតាខ្មៅ

glue gao; jor gao ការ; ជំរការ

go dtou ទៅ

go away! jeuñ dtou! ចេញទៅ!

go back (reverse) toy ថយ

goal *(aim)* goal bom-norng គោលបំណង

God bpray-ah ព្រះ

gold mee-ah មាស

goldsmith jee-ung mee-ah ជាងមាស

good la-or ល្អ

goodbye lee-a seun hai-ee លាសិនហើយ

good-natured s'loat la-or ស្លូតល្អ

gossip *(v)* nee-yay k'seup k'see-o និយាយខ្ញុបខ្ញៀរ

góvernment roa-ut-taa-pi-baal រដ្ឋាភិបាល

government official nay-uk roa-ut-ta-gaa អ្នករដ្ឋការ

governor *(provincial)* jao fai kait ចៅហ្វាយខេត្ត

grade t'nuk ថ្នាក់

graduate *(v)* ree-un jop; jop gaa seuk-saa រៀនចប់;
ចប់ការសិក្សា

grandchild jao ចៅ

granddaughter jao s'ray ចៅស្រី

grandfather *(paternal and maternal)* jee-dtaa; dtaa ជីតា;
តា

grandmother *(paternal and maternal)* jee-doan; yee-ay ជីដូន; យាយ

grandson   jao bproh   ចៅប្រុស

grape   dtom-bpay-ung bai joo   ទំពាំងបាយជូ

grass   s'mao   ស្មៅ

grateful   deung gOOn   ដឹងគុណ

grave (n)   p'noo   ផ្នូរ

grease (n)   kluñ   ខ្លាញ់

great-grandchild   jao dtoo-ut   ចៅទួត

great-grandfather   jee-dtaa dtoo-ut; dtaa dtoo-ut   ជីតាទួត; តាទួត

great-grandmother   jee-doan dtoo-ut; yee-ay dtoo-ut   ជីដូនទួត; យាយទួត

greedy   loap   លោភ

green   bai dtorng   បៃតង

greet   jOOm-ree-up soo-a   ជំរាបសួរ

grenade   kroa-up baik dai   គ្រាប់បែកដៃ

grey   bpra-peh   ប្រផេះ

ground   day   ដី

group   bpoo-uk; grom   ពួក; ក្រុម

grow *(plants)*   dum   ដាំ

   grow up   tom larng   ធំឡើង

guarantee (v)   rup-rorng; tee-a-nee-a   រ៉ាប់រង; ធានា

guard (n)   nay-uk yee-um   អ្នកយាម

guerrilla   dtoa-up ch'lorp   ទ័ពឈ្លប

guess (v)   s'maan   ស្មាន

guest   p'nyee-o   ភ្ញៀវ

guide (v)   deuk noa-um   ដឹកនាំ

tourist guide   mayk-gOO-dtayh dtay-sa-jor   មគ្គុទេសក៍
ទេសចរណ៍

guilty   mee-un dtoah   មានទោស

gun   gum-plerng   កាំភ្លើង

H

hair   sok   សក់

haircut   gut sok   កាត់សក់

half   gon-lah   កន្លះ

half an hour   gon-lah maong   កន្លះម៉ោង

hall *(pavilion)*   saa-laa   សាលា

hammer (n)   n'yor-n'yoo-a   ញញួរ

hammock   ong-reung   អង្រឹង

hand   dai   ដៃ

handbag   gra-boap yoo-a   ក្របូបយួរ

handicraft   seup-bpa-gum   សិប្បកម្ម

handle   dorng   ដង

handsome   sa-aat   ស្អាត

handwriting   jom-naa day   ចំណារដៃ

hang   bp'yoo-a   ព្យួរ

hanger *(for clothes)*   bpra-dup bp'yoo-a kao-ao   ប្រដាប់ព្យួរ
ខោអាវ

happen gart; gart larng កើត; កើតឡើង
  what's happening? gart mee-un reu'ung ay?
កើតមានរឿងអ្វី?
happy sop-bai សប្បាយ
harbor pai ផែ
hardly . . . meun sou . . . មិនសូវ . . .
harvest (v) *(rice)* j'root s'rou ច្រូតស្រូវ
hat moo-uk មួក
hate (v) sa-op ស្អប់
have mee-un មាន
  have a baby som-raal goan; gart goan សម្រាលកូន;
កើតកូន
  have a cold p'daa sai ផ្ដាសាយ
  have fun sop-bai reek ree-ay សប្បាយរីករាយ
  have to (must) dtrou ត្រូវ
he goa-ut គាត់
head *(body)* g'baal ក្បាល
  (leader) bpra-mOOk ប្រមុខ
headache cheu g'baal ឈឺក្បាល
headman may មេ
health sok-ka-pee-up សុខភាព
healthy mee-un sok-ka-pee-up la-or មានសុខភាពល្អ
hear leu; s'dup leu ឮ; ស្ដាប់ឮ
  I can't hear s'dup meun baan; s'dup meun leu
ស្ដាប់មិនបាន; ស្ដាប់មិនឮ

heart jeut ចិត្ត

heat gom-dao កំដៅ

heaven taan soo-a ឋានសួគិ

heavy t'ngoo-un ធ្ងន់

hell na-roo-uk នរក

hello jOOm-ree-up soo-a ជំរាបសួរ
   (on telephone) aa-loa អាឡូ

help (n) jOOm-noo-ay ជំនួយ

help (v) joo-ay ជួយ

hepatitis roak ra-lee-uk t'larm រោគរលាកថ្លើម

her goa-ut; nee-ung គាត់; នាង

here nih; ai nih នេះ; ឯនេះ

hero *(play, film)* dtoo-a aik bproh តួឯកប្រុស
   (war) wee-ray-a-bo-roh វីរបុរស

heroin aa-pee-un អាភៀន

heroine *(play, film)* dtoo-a aik s'ray តួឯកស្រី
   (war) wee-ray-a-sa-dtray វីរស្ត្រី

hide (v) lay-uk; bung លាក់; ប៉ាំង

high k'bpoo-ah ខ្ពស់

hill p'nOOm ភ្នំ

him goa-ut; wee-a គាត់; វា

hire joo-ul ជួល

his ra-boh goa-ut របស់គាត់

history bpra-woa-ut-ta-saah ប្រវត្តិសាស្ត្រ

hit (v) wee-ay វាយ

hoe (n) jorp ចប

hold gun កាន់

hole roong រូង

holiday t'ngai chOOp som-raak ថ្ងៃឈប់សម្រាក

home p'dtay-ah ផ្ទះ

homesick neuk p'dtay-ah; neuk s'rok នឹកផ្ទះ; នឹកស្រុក

honest dtee-ung dtrong; soch-ja-reut ទៀងត្រង់; សុច្ចរិត

honor geut-ta-yoo-ah កិត្តិយស

hope (v) song-keum សង្ឃឹម

lose hope oh song-keum អស់សង្ឃឹម

horse seh សេះ

hospital moo-un dtee bpairt មន្ទីរពេទ្យ

hot g'dao ក្តៅ

(spicy) heul; har ហិល; ហើរ

hotel son-ta-gee-a សណ្ឋាគារ

hour maong ម៉ោង

house p'dtay-ah ផ្ទះ

how yaang maych យ៉ាងម៉េច

how are you? sok sop-bai jee-a dtay? សុខសប្បាយជា
ទេ?

how much/many? bon-maan? ប៉ុន្មាន?

however yaang naa gor dao-ee យ៉ាងណាក៏ដោយ

hug aop reut ឱបរិត

huge tom som-barm ធំសម្បើម

human (n) ma-nOOh មនុស្ស

human rights   seut-ti ma-nOOh   សិទ្ធិមនុស្ស

humanitarian   ma-nOOh-sa-toa-a   មនុស្សធម៌

humanitarian aid   jOOm-noo-ay ma-nOOh- sa-toa-a
ជំនួយមនុស្សធម៌

humid   sarm   សើម

hundred   roy   រយ

hundred thousand   sain   សែន

hungry   klee-un   ឃ្លាន

hurry   bpra-n'yup   ប្រញាប់

hurt *(it hurts)*   cheu   ឈឺ

husband   b'day   ប្តី

hut   k'tOOm   ខ្ទម

I

I   k'nyom   ខ្ញុំ

ice   dteuk gork   ទឹកកក

ice cream   gaa-rem   ការ៉េម

idea   gOOm-neut   គំនិត

ideal (n)   OO-dom-ga-dte   ឧត្តមគតិ

identical   dor-dail   ដដែល

if   bar   បើ

ignore   t'wer t'long t'wer gor   ធ្វើថ្លង់ធ្វើតិ

ill   cheu   ឈឺ

illegal   koh ch'bup   ខុសច្បាប់

illness   jOOm-ngeu   ជម្ងឺ

imitate   dtrup; t'wer dtaam   ត្រាប់; ធ្វើតាម

immediately   plee-um   ភ្លាម

immigrant   nay-uk on-dtao bpra-wayh   អ្នកអន្តោប្រវេសន៍

impatient   k'mee-un om-not   គ្មានអំណត់

imperialism   juk-gra-bpoa-ut-nee-yOOm   ចក្រពត្តិនិយម

impolite   ot goo-a sorm   អត់គួរសម

import   noa-um joal   នាំចូល

important   som-kun   សំខាន់

impossible   k'mee-un plou neung t'wer baan   គ្មានផ្លូវនឹង
ធ្វើបាន

imprison   duk gOOk   ដាក់គុក

improve *(something)*   t'wer ao-ee bpra-sar larng   ធ្វើឲ្យ
ប្រសើរឡើង

in   k'nong   ក្នុង

  in order to   darm-bay neung   ដើម្បីនឹង

  in that case   bar doach-noh   បើដូច្នោះ

  in the process of   gom-bpOOng dtai   កំពុងតែ

incense   toop   ធូប

including   roo-um dtay-ung   រួមទាំង

increase (v)   dom-larng   តម្លើង

independence   aik-ga-ree-uch   ឯករាជ្យ

India   bpra-dtayh eun-dee-a   ប្រទេសឥណ្ឌា

Indochina   eun-doa-jeun   ឥណ្ឌូចិន

industry OO-saa-ha-gum ឧស្សាហកម្ម

informal *(unofficial)* grao plou-gaa ក្រៅផ្លូវការ

information dom-neung; bpoa-dta-mee-un ដំណឹង; ពត៌មាន

inject juk ចាក់

injustice a-yOOt-dta-toa-a អយុត្តិធម៌

ink dteuk k'mao ទឹកខ្មៅ

innocent *(not guilty)* k'mee-un'dtoah គ្មានទោស

insect sut la-eut សត្វល្អិត

inside kaang k'nong ខាងក្នុង

inspect dtroo-ut; bpi-neut ត្រួត; ពិនិត្យ

install duk; dom-larng ដាក់; តម្លើង

instead joo-ah ជួស

insult (v) dee-ul ជេរល

intelligent mee-un bpraach-n'yaa មានប្រាជ្ញា

intend geut គិត

intention jayt-dta-naa ចេតនា

intentionally dao-ee jayt-dta-naa ដោយចេតនា

interested jup jeut ចាប់ចិត្ត

interpreter nay-uk bork bprai អ្នកបកប្រែ

interrogate soo-a jom-lar-ee សួរចម្លើយ

intersection bpra-sop ប្រសព្វ

interview (n) som-pee-ah សម្ភាសន៍

interview (v) t'wer som-pee-ah ធ្វើសម្ភាសន៍

into k'nong ក្នុង

introduce noa-um s'koa-ul នាំស្គាល់

invade lOOk; rOOk ree-un លុក; រុករាន

invite (v) uñ-jerñ អញ្ជើញ

iron (steel) daik ដែក

irrigate bon-joal dteuk បញ្ចូលទឹក

is jee-a; geu ជា; គឺ

Islam eu-s'laam អ៊ីស្លាម

island goh កោះ

it wee-a វា

itch (v) ra-moa-ah រមាស់

J

jack (for lifting) daik kreep ដែកត្រីប

jackfruit k'nol (or k'nao) ខ្នុល

jail gOOk គុក

   to be in jail joa-up gOOk ជាប់គុក

   to put in jail duk gOOk ដាក់គុក

January mayk-ga-raa មករា

Japan jee-bpOOn ជីពុន; ជប៉ុន

jar (for storing water) bpee-ung ពាង

jaundice roak kun leu-ung រោគខាន់លឿង

jealous bpra-jun; j'ra-nain ប្រចណ្ឌ; ច្រណែន

jewelry kreu-ung a-long-gaa គ្រឿងអលង្ការ

job gaa ការ

join (v)   roo-um   រួម

joke (n)   reu-ung gom-bplaing   រឿងកំប្លែង

  I was joking   k'nyom ni-yee-ay gom-bplaing layng
  ខ្ញុំនិយាយកំប្លែងលេង

journalist   nay-uk gaa-sait   អ្នកកាសែត

journey   dom-nar   ដំណើរ

judge (n)   jao grom   ចៅក្រម

   (v)   gut k'day   កាត់ក្ដី

juice (*fruit juice*)   dteuk plai cher   ទឹកផ្លែឈើ

July   guk-ga-daa   កក្កដា

jump   loat   លោត

June   mi-to-naa   មិថុនា

jungle   bpray-ee   ព្រៃ

just (*fair*)   dtreum dtrou   ត្រឹមត្រូវ

just now   um-baañ meuñ   អម្បាញ់មិញ

  I have just . . .   k'nyom dterp dtai . . .   ខ្ញុំទើបតែ . . .

justice   yOOt-dta-toa-a   យុត្តិធម៌

K

Kampong Cham   gom-bpoo-ung jaam   កំពង់ចាម

Kampong Chhnang   gom-bpoo-ung ch'nung   កំពង់ឆ្នាំង

Kampong Speu   gom-bpoo-ung s'peu   កំពង់ស្ពឺ

Kampong Thom   gom-bpoo-ung tom   កំពង់ធំ

Kampot gom-bport កំពត

Kandal gon-daal កណ្ដាល

keep *(store, collect)* dtOOk ទុក

   keep out! gom joal កុំចូល

kerosene bprayng gaat ប្រេងកាត

kettle bpun-dtai ប៉ាន់តែ

key goan sao កូនសោ

Khmer k'mai ខ្មែរ

   Khmer Krom (ethnic Khmers from southern Vietnam)
   k'mai graom ខ្មែរក្រោម

kick dtoa-ut; tay-uk ទាត់; ធាក់

kill som-lup សម្លាប់

kilogram gee-loa-graam គីឡូក្រាម

kilometer gee-loa-mait គីឡូម៉ែត្រ

kind (n) yaang; baip; mOOk យ៉ាង; បែប; មុខ

king s'daich; ma-haa g'sut ស្ដេច; មហាក្សត្រ

kiss (v) tarp ថើប

kitchen p'dtay-ah bai ផ្ទះបាយ

kite k'laing bong-har ខ្លែងបង្ហោរ

   fly a kite bong-har k'laing បង្ហោរខ្លែង

knee joo-ung-goo-ung ជង្គង់

knife gum-beut កាំបិត

knock (v) (on a door) goo-ah (t'wee-a) គោះ (ទ្វារ)

know *(a person)* s'koa-ul ស្គាល់

   (how to do something) jeh ចេះ

(information) deung ដឹង

knowledge jom-neh jeh deung ចំណេះចេះដឹង

Koh Kong goh gong កោះកុង

Kratié gra-jeh ក្រចេះ

L

label s'laak ស្លាក

laborer gum-ma-gor កម្មករ

lack (v) kwah ខ្វះ

lake beung បឹង

lamp (electric) jong-gee-ung ចង្កៀង

land (n) (ground, soil) day ដី

landlord m'jah p'dtay-ah ម្ចាស់ផ្ទះ

lane j'rork ច្រក

language pee-a-saa ភាសា

lantern goam គោម

Lao lee-ew លាវ

Laos bpra-dtayh lee-ew ប្រទេសលាវ

large tom ធំ

last (final) jong grao-ee; jong bom-pot ចុងក្រោយ; ចុងបំផុត

last month kai mOOn ខែមុន

last night yOOp meuñ យប់មិញ

last week aa-dteut mOOn អាទិត្យមុន

last (v) *(endure)* joa-up yoo ជាប់យូរ

late yeut យឺត

later *(subsequently)* grao-ee moak ក្រោយមក

launder *(wash and iron)* baok OOt បោកអ៊ុត

laundryman/laundress nay-uk doh lee-ung kao ao
អ្នកដុសលាងខោអាវ

law ch'bup ច្បាប់

lawn t'lee-a smao ផ្លាស្មៅ

lawyer may-tee-a-wee មេធាវី

lay *(something down)* duk ដាក់

lazy k'jeul ខ្ជិល

lead (n) *(metal)* som-nor សំណ

  (v) deuk noa-um ដឹកនាំ

leader nay-uk deuk noa-um អ្នកដឹកនាំ

leaf s'leuk cher ស្លឹកឈើ

leak (v) leuch លិច

learn ree-un រៀន

least *(smallest, minimum)* yaang dteuch bom-pot
យ៉ាងតិចបំផុត

  at least yaang dteuch nah យ៉ាងតិចណាស់

leather s'baik sut ស្បែកសត្វ

leave *(depart)* jaak-jeuñ ចាកចេញ

leave *(something)* dtOOk joal ទុកចោល

leech *(land)* dtee-uk ទាក

   (water) ch'lerng ឡើង

left *(opposite of right)* ch'wayng ឆ្វេង

   left-hand side kaang ch'wayng dai ខាងឆ្វេងដៃ

leftover nou sol នៅសល់

leg jerng ជើង

legal dtaam ch'bup; s'rorp ch'bup តាមច្បាប់; ស្របច្បាប់

lemon groach ch'maa ក្រូចឆ្មា

lend ao-ee k'jay ឱ្យខ្ចី

length *(of time)* ra-yay-a bpayl រយៈពេល

leprosy roak kloo-ung រោគឃ្លង់

less than ... teuch jee-ung ... តិចជាង ...

lesson may ree-un មេរៀន

let (v) *(allow)* ao-ee; u-nOOñ-n'yaat ao-ee ឱ្យ; អនុញ្ញាតឱ្យ

   (hire out, rent out) joo-ul ជួល

letter *(alphabet)* dtoo-a uk-sor តួអក្សរ

   (post) som-bot សំបុត្រ

lettuce saa-lut សាឡាត់

level (adj) s'mar; ree-up ស្មើ; រាប

library bun-naa-lai បណ្ណាល័យ

licence *(driving)* som-bot bark-bor roo-ut-yoo-un សំបុត្របើកបររថយន្ត

lid grorp; gOOm-rorp គ្រប; គំរប

lie (v) *(down)* dtOOm-rayt ទំរេត

   (tell a lie) go-hok; por កុហក; ភរ

life jee-weut ជីវិត

   way of life jee-wee-a pee-up ជីវភាព

lift (n) *(elevator)* joo-un-dar yoang ជណ្ដើរយោង

lift (v) lerk larng លើកឡើង

light (n) *(ray, beam)* bpoo-un-leu ពន្លឺ

   (in color) k'jay ខ្ជី

   (in weight) sraal ស្រាល

   (sunlight) bpoo-un-leu t'ngai ពន្លឺថ្ងៃ

   light from a lamp bpoo-un-leu jong-gee-ung
ពន្លឺចង្កៀង

light (v) *(a fire)* och plerng អុជភ្លើង

lightbulb om-bpool plerng; om-bpool jong-gee-ung
អំពូលភ្លើង; អំពូលចង្កៀង

lightening playk bon-dtoa ផ្លេកបន្ទោរ

like *(enjoy)* joal jeut ចូលចិត្ត

   (similar) doach; bpra-hail k'nee-a ដូច; ប្រហែលគ្នា

   like this; like that yaang nih; yaang nOOh យ៉ាងនេះ;
យ៉ាងនោះ

line k'sai ខ្សែ

lion seung; dtao សិង្ហ; តោ

lip(s) bor-boa moa-ut បបូរមាត់

liquor s'raa ស្រា

list (n) *(of names)* bun-jee ch'moo-ah បញ្ជីឈ្មោះ

   (of things) bun-jee ra-boh បញ្ជីរបស់

listen s'dup ស្ដាប់

liter leet លីត្រ

little dtoach តូច

   a little bit bon-dteuch; bon-dteuch bon-dtoa-ich បន្តិច;
បន្តិចបន្តួច

live (adj) nou roo-ah; nou mee-un jee-weut នៅរស់;
នៅមានជីវិត

live (v) nou នៅ

liver t'larm ថ្លើម

living room bon-dtOOp dtor-dtoo-ul p'nyee-o បន្ទប់ទទួល
ភ្ញៀវ

lizard *(small house lizard)* jeeng-jok ជីងចក់

load (n) bon-dtOOk បន្ទុក

load (v) p'dtOOk ផ្ទុក

loaf *(of bread)* dom ដុំ

located nou នៅ

lock (n) sao សោ

lock (v) juk sao ចាក់សោ

long *(size)* wairng វែង

   (time) yoo យូរ

   as long as dor raap naa ដរាបណា

look (at) merl មើល

   look out! bpra-yut ប្រយ័ត្ន

look (for) rork merl រកមើល

look (like) doach jee-a ដូចជា

loose *(fitting)* ra-lOOng រលុង

lose *(something)* but ប្រាត់

   (be defeated) juñ ចាញ់

    lose one's way woo-ung-wayng វង្វេង

loud klung ខ្លាំង

love (n) saych-g'day s'ra-luñ សេចក្ដីស្រឡាញ់

   (v) s'ra-luñ ស្រឡាញ់

lovely la-or ល្អ

low *(in height)* dtee-up ទាប

   (in price) taok ថោក

lower (v) (the price) boñ-joh (dtom-lai) បញ្ចុះ(តម្លៃ)

luck som-naang សំណាង

   good luck som-naang la-or សំណាងល្អ

lucky mee-un som-naang មានសំណាង

lunch bai t'ngai dtrong បាយថ្ងៃត្រង់

lung soo-ut សួត

M

machine maa-seen ម៉ាស៊ីន

mad *(angry)* keung ខឹង

   (crazy, insane) ch'goo-ut ឆ្គួត

made (of) t'wer bpee ធ្វើពី

magazine dtoa-a-sa-naa-wa-day ទស្សនាវដ្ដី

maid nay-uk bom-rar s'ray អ្នកបំរើស្រី

mail (n) som-bot សំបុត្រ

mail (v)   p'nyar som-bot   ផ្ញើរសំបុត្រ

   airmail   som-bot p'nyar dtaam jerng aa-gaah   សំបុត្រ
ផ្ញើរតាមជើងអាកាស

make   t'wer   ធ្វើ

malaria   jOOm-ngeu grOOn juñ   ជម្ងឺគ្រុនចាញ់

male (animal)   ch'moal   ឈ្មោល

   (human)   bproh   ប្រុស

man (male)   bproh   ប្រុស

   (human being)   ma-nOOh   មនុស្ស

manager   nay-uk gun gup gaa; nay-uk jut gaa
អ្នកកាន់កាប់ការ; អ្នកចាត់ការ

mango   s'wai   ស្វាយ

mangosteen   morng-kOOt   មង្ឃុត

manner (way)   ra-bee-up   របៀប

many   j'ram   ច្រើន

   how many?   bpon-maan?   ប៉ុន្មាន?

map   pain-dtee   ផែនទី

March   mee-nee-a   មីនា

market   p'saa   ផ្សារ

married   gaa hai-ee   ការហើយ

marry (to get married)   ree-up gaa   រៀបការ

marsh   wee-ul poo-uk   វាលភក់

mat (woven grass mat)   gon-dtayl   កន្ទេល

match   cher-gooh   ឈើគូស

mathematics   gay-a-neut-ta-saah   គណិតសាស្ត្រ

mattress bpook ពូក

may aach . . . baan អាច ... បាន

   may I . . . ? k'nyom . . . baan dtay? ខ្ញុំ ... បានទេ?

May OO-sa-pee-a ឧសភា

maybe bpra-hail ប្រហែល

me k'nyom ខ្ញុំ

meal aa-haa អាហារ

mean (*what does . . . mean?*) . . . mee-un nay doach m'daych?
. . . មានន័យដូចម្ដេច?

   what do you mean? loak jong taa yaang naa?
លោកចង់ថាយ៉ាងណា?

   loak taa nih mee-un nay yaang naa? លោកថា
នេះមានន័យយ៉ាងណា?

meaning nay; bom-norng ន័យ; បំណង

meaningless k'mee-un nay គ្មានន័យ

measure (v) woa-ah វាស់

meat saich សាច់

mechanic jee-ung maa-seen ជាងម៉ាស៊ីន

medal may-dai មេដៃយ

medicine t'num bpairt ថ្នាំពេទ្យ

medium (adj) gon-daal កណ្ដាល

meet joo-up ជួប

meeting (*conference*) bpra-jOOm ប្រជុំ

Mekong (river) (too-un-lay) may-gorng (ទន្លេ)មេគង្គ

melon (*watermelon*) oa-leuk ឪឡឹក

musk melon   dtror-sok-srou   ត្រសក់ស្រូវ

melt   rOOm-lee-ay   រំលាយ

member   sa-maa-jeuk   សមាជិក

member of parliament   sa-maa-jeuk sa-pee-a
សមាជិកសភា

menu   bun-na-rai mOOk m'hoap;   បណ្ណរាយមុខមួប;
dtaa-raang m'hoap   តារាងម្ហូប

merchandise   dtOOm-neuñ   ទំនិញ

merchant   ch'moo-uñ   ឈ្មួញ

merit *(Buddhist)*   bon   បុណ្យ

metal   loa-ha-tee-ut   លោហធាតុ

meter   mait   ម៉ែត្រ

midday   t'ngai dtrong   ថ្ងៃត្រង់

middle   gon-daal   កណ្ដាល

midnight   aa-tree-ut   អាធ្រាត្រ

might *(may)*   bpra-hail aach . . . baan   ប្រហែលអាច ... បាន

mile   mai   ម៉ៃ

milk   dteuk doh   ទឹកដោះ

millimeter   mee-lee-mait   មិលីម៉ែត្រ

million   lee-un   លាន

mind *(spirit)*   sa-dte   សតិ

mine *(possesive)*   ra-boh k'nyom   របស់ខ្ញុំ

mine (n) *(explosive)*   kroa-up meen   គ្រាប់មីន

(ore)   un-doang rai   អណ្ដូងរ៉ែ

mineral   ka-neuch   ខនិជ

minister   roa-ut-ta-moo-un-dtray   រដ្ឋមន្ត្រី

ministry   gra-soo-ung   ក្រសួង

minute   nee-a-dtee   នាទី

mirror   goñ-jok   កញ្ចក់

mischievous   ra-bpeul ra-bpoach   របិលរប៉ូច

miss (v) *(a bus)*   dtou meun dtoa-un   ទៅមិនទាន់

   (long for)   neuk ra-leuk   នឹករឭក

Miss   guñ-n'yaa   កញ្ញា

   miss home, be homesick   neuk s'rok; neuk p'dtay-ah   នឹកស្រុក; នឹកផ្ទះ

missing   but   បាត់

mistake   gom-hoh   កំហុស

   make a mistake   t'wer koh   ធ្វើខុស

misunderstand   yoo-ul koh   យល់ខុស

mixed   jom-roh   ចម្រុះ

model   baip   បែប

modern   dtOOm-nerp; sa-mai t'may   ទំនើប; សម័យថ្មី

moment   plairt   ភ្លែត

   wait a moment   jum moo-ay plairt   ចាំមួយភ្លែត

Monday   t'ngai jun   ថ្ងៃចន្ទ

Mondulkiri   mOOn-doo-ul-gi-ree   មណ្ឌលគីរី

money   bpruk; loo-ee   ប្រាក់; លុយ

monk   loak song   លោកសង្ឃ

   enter the monkhood   boo-ah   បួស

monkey   s'waa   ស្វា

month kai ខែ

monument a-nOO-saa-wa-ree អនុស្សាវរិយ៍

moon loak kai; bpray-ah jun លោកខែ; ព្រះចន្ទ

more dtee-ut ទៀត

  one more moo-ay dtee-ut មួយទៀត

  more than ... j'rarn jee-ung ... ច្រើនជាង ...

morning bpreuk ព្រឹក

  in the morning nou bpayl bpreuk នៅពេលព្រឹក

  this morning bpreuk nih ព្រឹកនេះ

mosquito mooh មូស

most *(majority)* pee-uk j'rarn ភាគច្រើន

  (superlative) j'rarn jee-ung gay ច្រើនជាងគេ

mostly j'rarn dtai ច្រើនតែ

mother m'dai; mai ម្ដាយ; ម៉ែ

mother-in-law m'dai k'mayk ម្ដាយក្មេក

motor maa-seen; kreu-ung yoo-un ម៉ាស៊ីន; គ្រឿងយន្ត

motorcycle moa-dtoa ម៉ូតូ

mountain p'nOOm ភ្នំ

mouse *(rat)* gon-dol កណ្ដុរ

moustache bpOOk moa-ut ពុកមាត់

mouth moa-ut មាត់

move *(house)* plah p'dtay-ah ផ្លាស់ផ្ទះ

  (something) joo-uñ-joon ជញ្ជូន

movement jorl-la-naa ចលនា

  resistance movement jorl-la-naa dtor soo ចលនាតស៊ូ

movie gon; pee-up-yoo-un កុន; ភាពយន្ត
  to see a movie merl gon មើលកុន
Mr. loak លោក
Mrs. loak s'ray លោកស្រី
much j'ram ច្រើន
  too much j'ram bpayk ច្រើនពេក
mud poo-uk ភក់
multiply gOOn គុណ
murder (n) kee-a-ta-gum ឃាតកម្ម
  (v) som-lup សម្លាប់
murderer kee-a-ta-gor ឃាតករ
museum saa-ra-moo-un-dtee សារមន្ទីរ
mushroom p'seut ផ្សិត
music playng; don-dtray ភ្លេង; ដន្ត្រី
must dtrou ត្រូវ
my ra-boh k'nyom របស់ខ្ញុំ
myself kloo-un k'nyom; kloo-un aing ខ្លួនខ្ញុំ; ខ្លួនឯង

N

nail (n) daik goal ដែកគោល
naked aa-graat; kloo-un dtor-dtay អាក្រាត; ខ្លួនទទេ
name (n) ch'moo-ah ឈ្មោះ
  nickname ch'moo-ah hao grao ឈ្មោះហៅក្រៅ

    surname nee-um dtra-goal   នាមត្រកូល

namely geu គឺ

narcotics kreu-ung n'yee-un គ្រឿងញៀន

narrow jong-ee-ut ចង្អៀត

nation jee-ut; bpra-jee-a-jee-ut ជាតិ; ប្រជាជាតិ

nationalism jee-ut nee-yOOm ជាតិនិយម

nationality soñ-jee-ut; joo-un-jee-ut សញ្ជាតិ; ជនជាតិ

nature *(natural world)* toa-um-a-jee-ut ធម្មជាតិ

naughty ra-bpeul ra-bpoach របិលរប៉ូច

navy gorng dtoa-up jerng dteuk កងទ័ពជើងទឹក

near jeut; g'bai ជិត; ក្បែរ

nearly ster tai ស្ទើរតែ

neat sa-aat baat ស្អាតបាត

necessary jum-baich ចាំបាច់

neck gor ក

necklace k'sai gor ខ្សែក

necktie graa-wut ក្រវ៉ាត់

need (to) dtrou-gaa ត្រូវការ

    there's no need meun dtrou-gaa; meun jum-baich

  មិនត្រូវការ; មិនចំបាច់

needle m'jOOl ម្ជុល

neighbor nay-uk jeut kaang អ្នកជិតខាង

nephew k'moo-ay bproh ក្មួយប្រុស

nepotism kroo-a-saa nee-yOOm ត្រួសារនិយម

net *(mosquito)* mOOng មុង

never meun dail . . . មិនដែល ...

   never mind meun ay dtay មិនអ្វីទេ

new t'may ថ្មី

   brand new t'may s'ra-laang ថ្មីស្រឡាង

new year ch'num t'may ឆ្នាំថ្មី

news dom-neung; bpoa-daa-mee-un ដំណឹង; ពត៌មាន

newspaper gaa-sait កាសែត

next bon-dtoa-up បន្ទាប់

   next month kai grao-ee ខែក្រោយ

nice la-or ល្អ

niece k'moo-ay s'ray ក្មួយស្រី

night yOOp យប់

   last night yOOp meuñ យប់មិញ

nine bprum boo-un ប្រាំបួន

ninety gao seup កៅសិប

no dtay ទេ

nobody k'mee-un nor naa គ្មាននរណា

noise soa; som-layng សូរ; សម្លេង

noisy oo-ai; geuk gorng អូអែ; គឹកកង

noodles goo-ee dtee-o គុយទាវ

   egg noodles mee មី

noon t'ngai dtrong ថ្ងៃត្រង់

normal toa-um-a-daa ធម្មតា

north kaang jerng ខាងជើង

northeast kaang jerng chee-ung kaang gart ខាងជើង

ឆៀងខាងកើត

northwest kaang jerng chee-ung kaang leuch ខាងជើង
ឆៀងខាងលិច

nose j'ra-moh ច្រមុះ

not dtay ទេ

   not at all (you're welcome) meun ay dtay មិនអ្វីទេ

   not have k'mee-un គ្មាន

   not necessary meun jum-baich មិនចំបាច់

   not very . . . meun sou . . . មិនសូវ ...

   not . . . yet meun dtoa-un . . . dtay មិនទាន់ ... ទេ

notebook see-o pou sor-say សៀវភៅសរសេរ

nothing k'mee-un ay dtay គ្មានអ្វីទេ

notice (n) bpra-gaah ប្រកាស

notice (v) song-gayt សង្កេត

November weuch-a-gaa វិច្ឆិកា

now ay-lou nih ឥឡូវនេះ

nowadays sop t'ngai nih សព្វថ្ងៃនេះ

number *(figure)* layk លេខ

   (quantity) jom-noo-un ចំនួន

   telephone number layk dtoo-ra-sup លេខទូរស័ព្ទ

nun doan jee ដូនជី

nurse *(female)* gi-lee-un up-bpa-taa-yi-gaa
គិលានុបដ្ឋាយិកា

   (male) gi-lee-un up-bpa-taak គិលានុបដ្ឋាក

nut *(edible)*   kroa-up   ត្រាប់
   (for bolt)   g'baal lao see   ក្បាលឡៅស៊ី

O

obligation   gaa-dtup-bpa-geuch   កាតព្វកិច្ច
observe   song-gayt   សង្កេត
observer   nay-uk song-gayt gaa   អ្នកសង្កេតការ
obstacle   OOp-bpa-suk   ឧបសគ្គ
occupation   mOOk ra-bor   មុខរបរ
occupied *(busy, not free)*   joa-up ra-woo-ul; k'mee-un dtOOm-
   nay   ជាប់រវល់; គ្មានទំនេរ
occur   gart larng   កើតឡើង
ocean   ma-haa sa-mot   មហាសមុទ្រ
October   dto-laa   តុលា
of   ra-boh   របស់
office   dtee jut gaa; ga-ri-yaa-lai   ទិចាត់ការ; ការិយាល័យ
officer *(military)*   nee-ay dtee-a-hee-un   នាយទាហាន
official (adj)   plou gaa   ផ្លូវការ
official (n)   p'nay-uk ngee-a   ភ្នាក់ងារ
   government official   p'nay-uk ngee-a roa-ut-ta-baal
   ភ្នាក់ងាររដ្ឋបាល
often   n'yeuk n'yoa-up   ញឹកញ្យាប់

oil *(n)* bprayng ប្រេង
   cooking oil kluñ j'rook ខ្លាញ់ជ្រូក
   motor oil bprayng ប្រេង
oil *(v)* *(lubricate)* duk bprayng ដាក់ប្រេង
O.K. oa-kay អូខេ
old *(things, people)* jah ចាស់
   how old are you? aa-yOO bpon-maan hai-ee?
អាយុប៉ុន្មានហើយ?
older *(older brother)* borng bproh បងប្រុស
   older sister borng s'ray បងស្រី
on nou ler នៅលើ
   on the part of ai ... weuñ ង...វិញ
once *(one time)* m'dorng ម្ដង
   at once plee-um ភ្លាម
   once in a while yoo yoo m'dorng យូរៗ ម្ដង
   once more m'dorng dtee-ut ម្ដងទៀត
one moo-ay មួយ
oneself kloo-un aing ខ្លួនឯង
onion k'dteum baa-rung ខ្ទឹមបារាំង
   spring onion s'leuk k'dteum ស្លឹកខ្ទឹម
only dtai ... bon-noh; kroa-un dtai តែ...ប៉ុណ្ណោះ; គ្រាន់តែ
open bark បើក
   bottle opener kreu-ung bark dorp គ្រឿងបើកដប
operation *(surgical)* gaa way-ah gut ការវះកាត់
opinion yoa-bol យោបល់

opium aa-pee-un អាភៀន

opportunity ao-gaah ឱកាស

oppose dtor dtoo-ul តទល់

opposite dtoo-ul mOOk; kaang m'kaang ទល់មុខ; ខាងម្ខាង

oppress song-got song-geun; jih joa-un សង្កត់សង្កិន; ជិះជាន់

or reu ឬ

orange *(color)* bpoa-a leu-ung ពណ៌លៀង
   (fruit) groach bpoa-sut ក្រូចពោធិសាត់
   orange juice dteuk groatch ទឹកក្រូច

orchestra woo-ung playng; woo-ung don-dtray វង់ភ្លេង; វង់ដន្ត្រី

order (n) boñ-jee-a បញ្ជា

order (v) boñ-jee-a បញ្ជា
   in order to darm-bay neung ដើម្បីនឹង

ordinary toa-um-a-daa ធម្មតា

ore rai រ៉ែ

organize ree-up jum bong-gart រៀបចំបង្កើត

organization ong-gaa អង្គការ

origin gom-nart; darm-hait កំណើត; ដើមហេតុ

other ai dtee-ut ឯទៀត

ought goo-a dtai គួរតែ

our(s) ra-boh yerng របស់យើង

out *(go out)* jeuñ dtou grao ចេញទៅក្រៅ

outside kaang grao ខាងក្រៅ

oven lor ឡ

over *(above)* ler លើ

over *(finished)* jop hai-ee ចប់ហើយ

   (more than) lerh jee-ung លើសជាង

   (too much) j'rarn hoo-ah ច្រើនហួស

overthrow dtOOm-lay-uk; rOOm-lOOm ទម្លាក់; រំលំ

owe jOOm-bpay-uk ជំពាក់

owing (to) dao-ee hait dtai ដោយហេតុតែ

own *(self)* kloo-un aing ខ្លួនឯង

own *(v)* jee-a m'jah (ler) ជាម្ចាស់(លើ)

owner m'jah ម្ចាស់

ox goa ch'moal គោឈ្មោល

oyster k'yorng s'meut; ngee-o ខ្យងស្មឹត; ងាវ

P

package goñ-jop កញ្ចប់

paddy field s'rai ស្រែ

padlock sao dtra-daok សោត្រដោក

page dtOOm-bpoa-a ទំព័រ

pail *(for water)* tOOng dteuk ធុងទឹក

pain cheu ឈឺ

paint (n) t'num lee-up ថ្នាំលាប

paint (v) *(a house)* lee-up bpoa-a លាបពណ៌

  (a picture) goo គូរ

painter *(artist)* jee-ung gOOm-noo ជាងគូរគំនូរ

  (house) jee-ung lee-up (p'dtay-ah) ជាងលាប(ផ្ទះ)

painting *(picture)* gOOm-noo គំនូរ

pair goo គូ

palace way-ung វាំង

pan *(frying)* k'dtay-ah ខ្ទះ

pants *(trousers)* kao ខោ

  (underpants) kao k'nong ខោក្នុង

papaya l'hong ល្ហុង

paper gra-daah ក្រដាស

parents oa-bpOOk m'dai ឪពុកម្ដាយ

park (n) soo-un សួន

park (v) *(a car)* jort (laan) ចត (ឡាន)

parliament sa-pee-a jee-ut សភាជាតិ

part pee-uk; p'naik; jom-naik ភាគ; ផ្នែក; ចំណែក

partly ... partly ... m'yaang ... m'yaang ...
ម្យ៉ាង...ម្យ៉ាង...

party *(celebration)* bpaa-dtee ប៉ារទី

  (political) gay-a-na bpuk គណៈបក្ស

pass *(an exam)* joa-up ជាប់

  (go past) dtou hoo-ah ទៅហួស

  (overtake) waa វ៉ា

passenger nay-uk dom-nar អ្នកដំណើរ

passport li-keut ch'lorng dain លិខិតឆ្លងដែន

past *(previous)* mOOn មុន

path plou ផ្លូវ

patience om-not អំណត់

patient (adj) jeh ot too-un; mee-un om-not ចេះអត់ធន់;
មានអំណត់

patient (n) nay-uk jOOm-ngeu អ្នកជម្ងឺ

pay (v) bong t'lai បង់ថ្លៃ

pay (n) *(salary)* bpruk kai ប្រាក់ខែ

payment gaa bong bpruk ការបង់ប្រាក់

peace son-dti-pee-up សន្តិភាព
  peace-keeping force gorng ray-uk-saa son-dti-pee-up
  កងរក្សាសន្តិភាព
  peace talks gaa jor-jaa son-dti-pee-up ការចរចាសន្តិភាព

peanut son-daik day សណ្តែកដី

pearl (t'boang) gOOch k'yorng (គ្យង)គុចខ្យង

peasant nay-uk s'rai អ្នកស្រែ

peel (n) som-bork សបក
  (v) bork; jeut បក; ចិត

pen *(enclosure)* dtrOOng ទ្រុង
  (for writing) bpaa-gaa ប៉ាកា

pencil k'mao dai ខ្មៅដៃ

penis leung លិង្គ

people bpra-jee-a-joo-un ប្រជាជន

pepper *(green)* m'dtayh plaok ម្ទេសផ្លោក

percent   pee-uk roy   ភាគរយ

   15 percent   dop bprum pee-uk roy   ដប់ប្រាំភាគរយ

perfume   dteuk op   ទឹកអប់

perhaps   bpra-hail   ប្រហែល

period *(menstrual)*   ra-dou   រដូវ

permission   saych-g'day a-nOOñ-n'yaat   សេចក្ដីអនុញ្ញាត

permit (v)   a-nOOñ-n'yaat ao-ee   អនុញ្ញាតឲ្យ

person   ma-nOOh   មនុស្ស

personal   p'dtoa-ul kloo-un   ផ្ទាល់ខ្លួន

personality   reuk-bpee-a   បុកពា

perspiration   n'yerh   ញើស

perspire   baik n'yerh; jeuñ n'yerh   បែកញើស;ចេញញើស

petrol   bprayng sung   ប្រេងសាំង

pharmacy   p'dtay-ah loo-uk t'num bpairt; ao-sot-s'taan   ផ្សះលក់ថ្នាំពេទ្យ; ឱសថស្ថាន

Phnom Penh   p'nOOm bpeuñ   ភ្នំពេញ

photocopy (v)   tort aik-ga-saa   ថតឯកសារ

photograph (n)   roop tort   រូបថត

   to take a photograph   tort roop   ថតរូប

photographer   jee-ung tort roop   ជាងថតរូប

phrase   klee-a   ឃ្លា

pick *(out)*   rerh   រើស

   (someone up)   dtor-dtoo-ul   ទទួល

   (something up)   lark   លើក

pickle (v)   j'roo-uk   ជ្រក់

pickled vegetables bon-lai j'roo-uk បន្លែជ្រក់

picture roop; gOOm-noo រូប; គំនូរ

   (painting) gOOm-noo គំនូរ

   (photograph) roop tort រូបថត

piece dom ដុំ

pier pai; gom-bpoo-ung pai ផែ; កំពង់ផែ

pig j'rook ជ្រូក

pile (n) gOOm-nor គំនរ

   (v) gor គរ

pill t'num kroa-up; t'num layp ថ្នាំគ្រាប់; ថ្នំលេប

pillow k'nar-ee ខ្នើយ

pimple mOOn មុន

pin m'jOOl មួល

   safety pin m'jOOl k'dtoa-ah មួលខ្លាស់

pineapple m'noa-ah ម្នាស់

ping-pong bpeeng bpong ពីងប៉ុង

pink see jom-bpoo; p'gaa chook ស៊ីជម្ពូ; ផ្កាឈូក

pistol gum-plerng klay កាំភ្លើងខ្លី

pity may-dtaa មេត្តា

   what a pity! s'dai mairn; s'dai nah ស្តាយមែន; ស្តាយណាស់

place (n) gon-laing កន្លែង

   (v) duk dtOOk ដាក់ទុក

plan (n) pain-gaa; gOOm-roang gaa ផែនការណ៍; គម្រោងការណ៍

(v) kroang; gOOm-roang   ត្រោង; គម្រោង

plant (v) dum   ដាំ

plantation jom-gaa   ចំការ

plastic bplaa-s'teek   ប្លាស្ទិក

plate jaan   ចាន

plateau k'bpoo-ung ree-up   ខ្ពង់រាប

play (n) l'kaon   ល្ខោន

play (v) layng   លេង

  play cards layng bee-a   លេងបៀ

pleasant   jee-a dtee sop-bai; jee-a dtee bpeuñ jeut
  ជាទីសប្បាយ; ជាទីពេញចិត្ត

please *(invitation)* un-jerñ   អញ្ជើញ

  (request) soam   សូម

  please close the door   soam bpeut t'wee-a   សូមបិទទ្វា

  please come in   un-jerñ joal moak   អញ្ជើញចូលមក

please (v) bom-bpeuñ jeut   បំពេញចិត្ត

  please yourself (it's up to you)   dtaam dtai loak   តាមតែ
  លោក

pliers dorng-gup   ដង្កាប់

plow (n) nay-ung-goa-ul   នង្គ័ល

plow (v) p'joo-a   ភ្ជួរ

plug *(wash basin)* ch'nok   ឆ្នុក

  (electric) bpra-dup sork   ប្រដាប់សិក

plumber   jee-ung dtor bom-bpoo-ung dteuk
  ជាងតបំពង់ទឹក

pocket   hao bpou   ហោប៉ៅ

poet   ga-way   កវី

point (at)   jong-ol   ចង្អុល

pointed *(sharp)*   s'roo-uch   ស្រួច

poison   t'num bom-bpOOl; t'num bpOOl   ថ្នាំបំពុល;
ថ្នាំពុល

poisonous   mee-un bpeuh; bpol   មានពិស; ពុល

police, policeman   dtom-roo-ut; bpoa-leeh   តម្រួត; ប៉ូលីស

policy   ne-yoa-bai   នយោបាយ

polite   goo-a sorm; jeh goo-a sorm   គួរសម; ចេះគួរសម

politician   nay-uk ne-yoa-bai   អ្នកនយោបាយ

politics   ne-yoa-bai   នយោបាយ

pomelo   groach k'weuch   ក្រូចឃ្វិច

pond *(large)*   s'rah   ស្រះ

   (small)   dtra-bpay-ung   ត្រពាំង

pool *(swimming)*   aang hail dteuk   អាងហែលទឹក

poor   gror; gray gror   ក្រ; ក្រីក្រ

population   bpra-jee-joo-un   ប្រជាជន

pork   saich j'rook   សាច់ជ្រូក

port   pai; gom-bpoo-ung pai   ផែ; កំពង់ផែ

post *(position, job)*   dtom-naing   តំណែង

   (stake)   bong-goal   បង្គោល

postcard   bprai-sa-nee-ya-bot   ប្រៃសណីយបត្រ

postman   nay-uk jaik som-bot   អ្នកចែកសំបុត្រ

post office   bprai-sa-nee-ya-taan   ប្រៃសណីយដ្ឋាន

pot *(cooking)* ch'nung day ឆ្នាំងដៃ

potato dom-loang ដំឡូង

pound (v) dom ដំ

pour juk ចាក់

poverty pee-up gror ភាពក្រ

poverty-stricken gror lOOm-baak ក្រលំបាក

powder m'sao ម្សៅ
  face powder m'sao lee-up mOOk ម្សៅលាបមុខ
  powdered milk m'sao dteuk doh goa ម្សៅទឹកដោះគោ

power *(energy, strength)* gom-lung កម្លាំង
  (influence) om-naich អំណាច

practice (v) hut ហាត់

prawn bong-gorng បង្គង

Preah Vihear bpray-ah wi-hee-a ព្រះវិហារ

precious stone t'boang ត្បូង

pregnant mee-un p'dtay-ee bpoo-ah; mee-un dtOOm-ngoo-
  un មានផ្ទៃពោះ; មានទម្មន់

prepare bom-rong; ree-up jom បំរុង; រៀបចំ

present *(at present)* ay-lou nih ឥឡូវនេះ

present (n) jOOm-noon; gaa-doa ជំនូន; កាដូ

president *(chairman)* bpra-tee-un ប្រធាន
  (of a country) bpra-tee-a-nee-a-teu-ba-day
  ប្រធានាធិបតី

pretty la-or; la-or sa-aat ល្អ; ល្អស្អាត

prevent bong-gaa បង្ការ

previous mOOn; bpee mOOn មុន; ពីមុន
Prey Veng pray-ee wairng ព្រៃវែង
price dtom-lai; t'lai តម្លៃ; ថ្លៃ
priest loak song លោកសង្ឃ
primary education bpa-tom seuk-saa បឋមសិក្សា
prime minister nee-a-yoak roa-ut-ta-moo-un-dtray
   នាយករដ្ឋមន្ត្រី
print (v) boh bpOOm បោះពុម្ព
prison gOOk គុក
prisoner nay-uk dtoah អ្នកទោស
private aik-ga-joo-un; soo-un dtoo-a; p'dtoa-ul kloo-un
   ឯកជន; សួនតូ; ផ្ទាល់ខ្លួន
   private ownership gum-ma-seut soo-un dtoo-a
   កម្មសិទ្ធិសួនតូ
privilege aik-ga-seut ឯកសិទ្ធិ
prize rorng-woa-un រង្វាន់
probably mOOk jee-a មុខជា
problem bpuñ-n'ya-haa បញ្ហា
procession g'boo-un hai ក្បួនហែ
produce (v) t'wer; pol-leut ធ្វើ; ផលិត
profession mOOk ra-bor មុខរបរ
professor saa-straa-jaa សាស្ត្រាចារ្យ
profit gom-rai កំរៃ
progress (n) woa-ut-ta-na-pee-up វឌ្ឍនភាព
   (v) jom-rarn ចំរើន

prohibit   haam   ហាម

promise (n)   bpee-uk son-yaa   ពាក្យសន្យា

promise (v)   son-yaa   សន្យា

proof   poa-ah dtaang   ភស្តុតាង

propaganda   gaa koa-sa-naa   ការឃោសនា

proper   som-rOOm; dtreum dtrou   សមរម្យ; ត្រឹមត្រូវ

prostitute   s'ray koach; s'ray som-peung   ស្រីខូច;
ស្រីសំផឹង

protect   goa-um-bpee-a   កាំពារ

protest   dtor waa   តវ៉ា

proud (of)   bpeuñ jeut (neung)   ពេញចិត្ត (និង)
   (haughty, vain)   gaong   កោង

prove   bong-haañ poa-ah dtaang   បង្ហាញភស្តុតាង

province   kait   ខេត្ត

public (adj)   saa-tee-a-ra-nah   សាធារណៈ
   public health   saa-tee-a-ra-nah-sok-kaa-pi-baal
សាធារណៈសុខាភិបាល
   (n)   bpra-jee-a-joo-un   ប្រជាជន

pull (v)   dtee-uñ   ទាញ

pull out *(withdraw)*   dork   ដក

pump (n)   kreu-ung boam   គ្រឿងបូម

pump (v)   boam   បូម

pumpkin   l'bpou   ល្ពៅ

punch (v)   dul   ដាល់

punish   duk dtoah; t'wer dtoah   ដាក់ទោស; ធ្វើទោស

pure sot-saat; bor-ri-sot សុទ្ធសាធ; បរិសុទ្ធ
purple bpoa-a s'wai ពណ៌ស្វាយ
purpose *(on purpose)* dao-ee jay-dta-naa ដោយចេតនា
Pursat bpoa-sut ពោធិសាត់
purse gaa-boap កាបូប
put duk ដាក់

Q

quality kOOn-na-pee-up គុណភាព
quantity jom-noo-un; bor-ri-maan ចំនួន; បរិមាណ
quarter moo-ay pee-uk boo-un មួយភាគបួន
queen bpray-ah ree-ich-a-nee ព្រះរាជនី
queer *(unusual)* bplaik; jom-laik ប្លែក; ចម្លែក
question (n) som-noo-a សំនួរ
   ask a question soo-a; t'wer som-noo-a សួរ; ធ្វើសំនួរ
quick ror-hah; chup; bpra-n'yup រហ័ស; ឆាប់; ប្រញាប់
quickly yaang ror-hah; chup យ៉ាងរហ័ស; ឆាប់
quiet *(silent)* s'ngut; s'ngut s'ngee-um ស្ងាត់;
   ស្ងាត់ស្ងៀម
   (tranquil) s'ngop s'ngut ស្ងប់ស្ងាត់
quit chOOp; lay-ah bong ឈប់; លះបង់
   quit a job chOOp bpee dtom-naing ឈប់ពីតំណែង

R

rabbit   dtoo-un-sai   ទន្សាយ

rabies   roak klaich dteuk; jOOm-ngeu ch'gai ch'goo-ut
រោគខ្លាចទឹក; ជម្ងឺឆ្កែឆ្កួត

race (n) *(nationality)*   saah; jee-ut saah; bpooch
សាសន៍;ជាតិសាសន៍;ពូជ

race (v)   bpra-nung   ប្រណាំង

   horse race   bpra-nung seh   ប្រណាំងសេះ

racetrack   plou bpra-nung   ផ្លូវប្រណាំង

radio   wit-yOO   វិទ្យុ

rag   gon-dtorp   កន្ទប់

railway   plou ra-dtayh plerng   ផ្លូវរទេះភ្លើង

rain (n, v)   plee-ung   ភ្លៀង

raincoat   ao plee-ung   អាវភ្លៀង

raise (v)   lerk   លើក

   raise prices   dom-larng t'lai   ដំឡើងថ្លៃ

rake (n)   ra-noa-ah   រនាស់

rambutan   sao-mao   សាវម៉ាវ

rank   joa-un; t'nuk   ជាន់; ថ្នាក់

rape (v)   jup rOOm-loap s'ray   ចាប់រំលោបស្រី

rare   gom-ror mee-un   កម្រមាន

rat   gon-dol   កណ្ដុរ

Ratanakiri roat-ta-na-gi-ree រតនៈគីរី

rate ut-dtraa អត្រា

rattan p'dao ផ្តៅ

raw *(uncooked)* chao ឆៅ

razor gom-beut gao កាំបិតកោរ

   razor blade plai gom-beut gao ផ្លែកាំបិតកោរ

reach *(arrive)* dol ដល់

   (with one's hand) choang ឈោង

read merl; aan មើល; អាន

ready ree-up jom hai-ee រៀបចំហើយ

real *(genuine, authentic)* sot សុទ្ធ

   (true) bpeut; mairn dtairn ពិត; មែនទែន

   really? mairn reu? មែនឬ?

reason hait ហេតុ

   for this reason dao-ee hait nih ដោយហេតុនេះ

receipt bong-gun dai បង្កាន់ដៃ

receive dtor-dtoo-ul ទទួល

recently t'may t'may nih ថ្មី ៗ នេះ

recommend s'nar ស្នើរ

record (n) *(background)* bpra-woa-ut ប្រវត្តិ

   (note) buñ-jee gum-not បញ្ជីកំណត់

record (v) *(note)* got dtOOk កត់ទុក

   (sound) tort som-layng ថតសម្លេង

red gra-horm ក្រហម

Red Cross gaak-ga-baat gra-horm កាកបាតក្រហម

reduce bon-toy; bon-joh បន្ថយ; បញ្ចុះ
   reduce the price bon-joh t'lai បញ្ចុះថ្លៃ
refrigerator dtoo dteuk gork ទូទឹកកក
refugee joo-un pee-ah kloo-un ជនភៀសខ្លួន
refugee camp jOOm-rOOm joo-un pee-ah kloo-un
   ជំរំជនភៀសខ្លួន
refuse (v) meun bprorm; bpa-de-sayt មិនព្រម; បដិសេធ
regard (as) jut dtOOk jee-a ចាត់ទុកជា
regarding *(about)* jom-bpoo-ah; om-bpee; s'day bpee
   ចំពោះ; អំពី; ស្ដីពី
region dtom-born តំបន់
register (v) joh buñ-jee ចុះបញ្ជី
regular dtee-ung dtoa-ut ទៀងទាត់
regulation bot boñ-jee-a បទបញ្ញា
reject (v) j'raan jaol ច្រានចោល
relative *(kin)* n'yee-ut son-daan ញាតិសន្ដាន
relax bon-too aa-rom បន្ទូអារម្ម
release doh lairng ដោះលែង
religion saa-s'naa សាសនា
remember jum ចាំ
remind rOOm-leuk រំលឹក
remove yoak jeuñ យកចេញ
rent (n) ch'noo-ul · ឈ្នួល
rent (v) joo-ul ជួល
repair (v) joo-ah jol ជួសជុល

repeat (v)   t'wer m'dorng dtee-ut   ធ្វើម្តងទៀត

   please repeat that (say again)   soam taa m'dorng dtee-ut
សូមថាម្តងទៀត

report (v)   ree-ay gaa   រាយការណ៍

representative   nay-uk dom-naang   អ្នកដំណាង

request (v)   som; soam   សុំ; សូម

require   dtrou-gaa   ត្រូវការ

requirement   saych g'day dtrou-gaa   សេចក្តីត្រូវការ

research (v)   s'rao j'ree-o   ស្រាវជ្រាវ

reserve (v)   bom-rong dtOOk   បម្រុងទុក

resign   lee-a jeuñ bpee dtom-naing   លាចេញពីតំណែង

respect (v)   goa-rOOp   គោរព

   show respect   som-daing saych-g'day goa-rOOp
សំដែងសេចក្តីគោរព

responsibility   gaa dtor-dtoo-ul koh dtrou
ការទទួលខុសត្រូវ

responsible   dtor-dtoo-ul koh dtrou   ទទួលខុសត្រូវ

rest (v)   som-raak   សម្រាក

restaurant   haang bai; poa-cha-nèe-ya-taan   ហាងបាយ;
ភោជនីយដ្ឋាន

retire   joal ni-woa-ut   ចូលនិវត្ត

return *(come back)*   dtra-lop moak   ត្រឡប់មក

   (give back)   joon dtou weuñ   ជូនទៅវិញ

   (go back)   dtra-lop dtou   ត្រឡប់ទៅ

revolution   bpa-de-woa-ut   បដិវត្តន៍

reward rorng-woa-un រង្វាន់

rhythm jong-wuk ចង្វាក់

rice (*cooked*) bai បាយ

   (*husked*) ong-gor អង្ករ

   (*unhusked*) s'rou ស្រូវ

   fried rice bai chaa បាយឆា

rice farmer nay-uk s'rai អ្នកស្រែ

rice field s'rai ស្រែ

rice gruel bor-bor បបរ

rich (*wealthy*) mee-un មាន

   the rich nay-uk mee-un អ្នកមាន

ride (v) jih ជិះ

rifle gum-plerng wairng កាំភ្លើងវែង

right (*correct*) dtrou ត្រូវ

   (*opposite of left*) s'dum ស្ដាំ

   on the right-hand side nou kaang s'dum day

   នៅខាងស្ដាំដៃ

   right here dtrong nih ត្រង់នេះ

right (n) (*of ownership*) gum-ma-seut កម្មសិទ្ធិ

ring (n) (*jewelry*) jeuñ-jee-un ចិញ្ចៀន

ring (v) (*a bell*) ong-rOOn gon-deung អ្រ្គនកណ្ដឹង

ripe dtOOm ទុំ

rise graok; lamg ក្រោក; ឡើង

river dtoo-un-lay ទន្លេ

   Mekong River dtoo-un-lay may-gong ទន្លេមេកុង

road plou; t'nol ផ្លូវ; ថ្នល់

roast ung អាំង

rob bplon ប្លន់

robber jao ចោរ

rock t'mor ថ្ម

roof dom-boal ដំបូល

room bon-dtOOp បន្ទប់

rope k'sai ខ្សែ

rose (n) p'gaa goa-laap ផ្កាកុឡាប

rot koach; ra-loo-ay; sa-oy ខូច; រលួយ; សួយ

rough *(uneven)* meun ree-up s'mar មិនរាបស្មើរ

round mool មូល

row (n) *(line)* joo-a ជួរ

  (quarrel) jom-loh ជម្លោះ

row (v) (a boat) om dtook អុំទូក

rubber gao soo កៅស៊ូ

rubber band woo-ung gao soo វង់កៅស៊ូ

ruby (t'boang) dta-dteum (ត្បូង)ទទឹម

rug bprOOm ព្រំ

ruin (v) *(destroy)* bom-plaañ បំផ្លាញ

ruins (n) *(ancient)* wi-geun-na-dtaan វិកិណ្ណដ្ឋាន

ruler *(for measuring)* bon-dtoa-ut បន្ទាត់

run roo-ut រត់

  (rivers) hoa ហូរ

  run away roo-ut jeuñ dtou រត់ចេញទៅ

Russia rOO-see រុស្ស៊ី

rust j'reh ច្រែះ

rusty j'reh jup; j'reh see ច្រែះចាប់; ច្រែះស៊ី

S

sack bao; gaa-rong; torng បាវ; ការុង; ថង់

sad bproo-ay; bproo-ay jeut ព្រួយ; ព្រួយចិត្ត

safe meun t'loh t'lao-ee; k'mee-un kroo-ah t'nuk មិនថ្លោះ
ថ្លាយ; គ្មានគ្រោះថ្នាក់

safety ni-ra-pay និរភ័យ

sailboat dtook g'daong ទូកក្តោង

sailor gum-ma̱-gor nee-a-wee-a កម្មករនាវា

salad saa-lut សាឡាត់

salary bpruk kai ប្រាក់ខែ

sale *(price reduction)* loo-uk joh t'lai លក់ចុះថ្លៃ
  for sale som-rup loo-uk សំរាប់លក់

salesman nay-uk loo-uk អ្នកលក់

salt om-beul អំបិល

salt water dteuk om-beul ទឹកអំបិល

salty bprai ប្រៃ

same dor-dail; doach k'nee-a ដដែល; ដូចគ្នា
  at the same time nou bpayl ji-moo-ay k'nee-a; k'nong
  bpayl dtai moo-ay នៅពេលជាមួយគ្នា; ក្នុងពេលតែមួយ

    exactly the same   doach k'nee-a sot saat   ដូចគ្នាសុទ្ធសាធ

    the same person   ma-nOOh doach k'nee-a; ma-nOOh dtai

    moo-ay   មនុស្សដូចគ្នា; មនុស្សតែមួយ

sample   dtom-naang; gOOm-roo   តំណាង; គំរូ

sand   day k'saich   ដីខ្សាច់

sanitary   a-naa-mai   អនាម័យ

satisfaction   saych g'day bpeuñ jeut   សេចក្ដីពេញចិត្ត

satisfactory   jee-a dtee bpeuñ jeut   ជាទីពេញចិត្ត

satisfied   bpeuñ jeut   ពេញចិត្ត

satisfy   bom-bpeuñ jeut   បពេញចិត្ត

Saturday   t'ngai sao   ថ្ងៃសៅរ៍

saucer   goan jaan dtee-up   កូនចានទាប

sausage   saich grork   សាច់ក្រក

save *(keep)*   son-som dtOOk   សន្សំទុក

   (rescue)   joo-ay song-kroo-ah   ជួយសង្រ្គោះ

   save money   son-som bpruk   សន្សំប្រាក់

saw (n)   ra-naa   រណារ

saw (v)   aa   អារ

say   ni-yee-ay taa   និយាយថា

scales *(for weighing)*   joo-uñ-jeeng   ជញ្ជីង

scarce   gror   ក្រ

scare (v)   bon-laich; bom-pay   បន្លាច; បំភ័យ

scared   pay; klaich   ភ័យ; ខ្លាច

scarf   gror-maa   ក្រមា

school   saa-laa ree-un   សាលារៀន

science wit-yee-a-saah វិទ្យាសាស្ត្រ

scientist nay-uk wit-yee-a-saah អ្នកវិទ្យាសាស្ត្រ

scissors gon-dtrai កន្ត្រៃ

scream s'raik ស្រែក

screen (n) *(window)* som-nuñ សំណាញ់

screw lao-see; k'jao ឡោស៊ី; ខ្ចៅ

screwdriver bpra-dup moo-ul lao-see ប្រដាប់មូលឡោស៊ី

script *(Cambodian script)* uk-sor k'mai អក្សរខ្មែរ

scrub doh joot; doh kut ដុសជូត; ដុសខាត់

sculpture roop jom-luk រូបចម្លាក់

sea sa-mot សមុទ្រ

seal (v) boh dtraa បោះត្រា

seashore moa-ut sa-mot មាត់សមុទ្រ

season ra-dou រដូវ

  cool season ra-dou ra-ngee-a រដូវរងា

  hot season ra-dou g'dao រដូវក្តៅ

  rainy season ra-dou plee-ung រដូវភ្លៀង

seat gon-laing ong-goo-ee កន្លែងអង្គុយ

second *(2nd)* dtee bpee ទីពីរ

  (unit of time) wi-nee-a-dtee វិនាទី

secondary education mut-t'yOOm seuk-saa មធ្យមសិក្សា

secret (adj) som-ngut សម្ងាត់

secret (n) gaa som-ngut ការសម្ងាត់

secretary lay-kaa-ti-gaa; s'mee-un លេខាធិការ; ស្មៀន

section pee-uk; p'naik ភាគ; ផ្នែក

see kern ឃើញ

seed(s) kroa-up bpooch គ្រាប់ពូជ

seek swaing rork ស្វែងរក

seem huk doach jee-a ហាក់ដូចជា

seldom ... meun sou ... មិនសូវ...

select rerh; j'rerh rerh; jom-ruñ រើស; ជ្រើសរើស; ចម្រាញ់

self kloo-un aing ខ្លួនឯង

selfish geut dtai kloo-un aing គិតតែខ្លួនឯង

sell loo-uk លក់

send p'nyar ផ្ញើរ

sentence *(grammar)* bpra-yoak ប្រយោគ

September guñ-n'yaa កញ្ញា

serious *(disposition)* meun layng sarch មិនលេងសើច

   (illness) t'ngoo-un ធ្ងន់

   (situation) don-daap ដុនដាប

servant nay-uk bom-rar អ្នកបម្រើ

serve bom-rar បម្រើ

service gaa bom-rar ការបម្រើ

set (n) *(of items)* chOOt; som-rup ឈុត; សម្រាប

seven bprum bpee ប្រាំពីរ

seventy dop bprum bpee ដប់ប្រាំពីរ

several bay boo-un បីបួន

sew day ដេរ

sewage dteuk som-oo-ee ទឹកសំអុយ

sewing machine   maa-seen day   ម៉ាស៊ីនដេរ

shade   m'lop   ម្លប់

   in the shade   k'nong m'lop   ក្នុងម្លប់

shadow   s'ra-maol   ស្រមោល

shallow *(water)*   ray-uk   រាក់

shampoo (n)   t'num gok   ថ្នាំកក់

shampoo (v)   gok sok   កក់សក់

shape   ree-ung; dtroo-ung dtree-ay; roop ree-ung   រាង;
ទ្រង់ទ្រាយ; រូបរាង

sharp *(pointed)*   s'roo-uch; mOOt   ស្រួច; មុត
   ten o'clock sharp   nou maong dop got   នៅម៉ោងដប់គត់

shave   gao bpOOk moa-ut   ការពុកមាត់

she   nee-ung; nay-uk s'ray; loak s'ray   នាង; អ្នកស្រី;
លោកស្រី

sheet   gom-raal grair dayk   កម្រាលគ្រែដេក

shelf   t'nar   ធ្នើរ

shell   k'yorng   ខ្យង

ship (n)   g'bul   កប៉ាល់

shirt   ao   អាវ

shoe(s)   s'baik jerng   ស្បែកជើង

shoelace   k'sai s'baik jerng   ខ្សែស្បែកជើង

shoot (v)   buñ   បាញ់

   shoot a gun   buñ gum-plerng   បាញ់កាំភ្លើង

shop (n)   haang   ហាង

shore *(seashore)*   moa-ut sa-mot   មាត់សមុទ្រ

short   klay   ខ្លី

   short (person)   dtee-up   ទាប

   in a short time   k'nong bpayl yaang klay   ក្នុង ពេលយ៉ាងខ្លី

shorts   kao klay   ខោខ្លី

should   goo-a dtai   គួរតែ

shout (v)   s'raik   ស្រែក

show (v)   bong-haañ   បង្ហាញ

show me *(demonstrate for me)*   t'wer ao-ee k'nyom merl   ធ្វើឱ្យខ្ញុំមើល

   (let me see)   ao-ee k'nyom merl; bong-haañ k'nyom   ឱ្យខ្ញុំមើល; បង្ហាញខ្ញុំ

   (point it out)   jong-ol ao-ee k'nyom merl   ចង្អុលឱ្យខ្ញុំមើល

shower *(take a bath)*   ngoot dteuk   ងូតទឹក

shrimp   bong-gorng   បង្គង

shut   bpeut   បិទ

shy   ee-un   អៀន

sick   cheu; meun sroo-ul kloo-un   ឈឺ; មិនស្រួលខ្លួន

side   kaang   ខាង

sidewalk   jeun-jarm t'nol   ចិញ្ចើមផ្លូវ

Siem Reap   see-um ree-up   សៀមរាប

sightseeing   gaa dar dtoa-a-sa-naa gom-saan   ការដើរទស្សនាកំសាន្ត

sign (n)   suñ-n'yaa   សញ្ញា

sign (v) *(one's name)* see-n'yay ស៊ីញ៉េ

silent s'ngee-um; s'ngut ស្ងៀម; ស្ងាត់

silk soot; bprair សូត្រ; ព្រៃ

silver bpruk ប្រាក់

silverware kreu-ung bpruk គ្រឿងប្រាក់

similar bpra-hail k'nee-a ប្រហែលគ្នា

simultaneously k'nong bpayl bprorm ji-moo-ay k'nee-a
ក្នុងពេលព្រមជាមួយគ្នា

since *(because)* dao-ee hait taa ដោយហេតុថា
  (from the time) dtung bpee តាំងពី

sing j'ree-ung ច្រៀង

singer nay-uk j'ree-ung អ្នកច្រៀង

single dtai moo-ay តែមួយ
  (unmarried) nou lew នៅលីវ

sister *(elder)* borng s'ray បងស្រី
  (younger) bpa-oan s'ray ប្អូនស្រី

sit ong-goo-ee អង្គុយ

sit down ong-goo-ee joh អង្គុយចុះ
  please sit down sohm un-jern ong-goo-ee សូម
  អញ្ជើញអង្គុយ

situated nou នៅ

situation *(state of affairs)* s'taan-na-gaa ស្ថានការណ៍

six bprum moo-ay ប្រាំមួយ

sixty hok seup ហុកសិប

size dtOOm-hOOm ទំហំ

skill gaa beun bpra-sop; gaa jOOm-nee-uñ ការបុិនប្រសប់; ការជំនាញ

skilled beun bpra-sop; bpoo-gai; jOOm-nee-uñ បុិនប្រសប់; ពូកែ; ជំនាញ

skin s'baik ស្បែក

skirt som-bpoo-ut សំពត់

sky mayk មេឃ

slap (v) dtay-ah ទះ

sleep (v) dayk; som-raan ដេក; សម្រាន្ត

sleepy ngor-ngoo-ee dayk ងុងុយដេក

slender s'rao ស្រាវ

slice (v) hun; jeut ហាន់; ចិត

slim (adj) ree-ung s'doo-ich រាងស្តូច

slippery ra-eul រអិល

slow yeut យឺត

slowly yeut yeut; moo-ay moo-ay យឺត ៗ; មួយ ៗ
  please speak slowly soam ni-yee-ay yeut yeut
  សូមនិយាយយឺត ៗ

small dtoa-ich តូច

smallpox ot-tom; p'gaa cher អុតធំ; ផ្កាឈើ

smart *(clever)* way-ee ch'laat; bpraach-n'yaa វៃឆ្លាត; ប្រាជ្ញា

smell (n) gleun ក្លិន
  have a nice smell gleun la-or; gleun gra-oap ក្លិនល្អ; ក្លិនក្រអូប

have a bad smell   gleun meun la-or; gleun aa-grok
ក្លិនមិនល្អ; ក្លិនអាក្រក់

smell delicious   ch'ngoo-ee   ឆ្ងុយ

smile (v)   n'yor-n'yeum   ញញឹម

smoke (n)   p'saing   ផ្សែង

smoke (v) (cigarette)   joo-uk (baa-ray)   ជក់(បារី)

smooth   ree-up   រាប

snake   bpoo-ah   ពស់

sneeze   gon-daah   កណ្ដាស់

snow (n)   bpreul   ព្រិល

so   doach nih   ដូច្នេះ

soap   saa-boo   សាប៊ូ

soccer   bul dtoa-ut   បាល់ទាត់

society   song-gOOm   សង្គម

sock(s)   s'raom jerng   ស្រោមជើង

soft   dtoo-un   ទន់

softly   yaang s'raal   យ៉ាងស្រាល

soldier   dtee-a-hee-un; yoa-tee-a; yoa-tin   ទាហាន; យោធា;
យោធិន

solution *(to problem)*   j'rork jeuñ; dom-noh s'rai   ច្រក
ចេញ; ដំណោះស្រាយ

solve *(a problem)*   doh s'rai bpuñ-n'ya-haa   ដោះ
ស្រាយបញ្ហា

some   klah   ខ្លះ

someone   nay-uk naa; nor naa   អ្នកណា; នរណា

something   a-way a-way   អ្វី ៗ

sometimes   joo-un gaal   ជួនកាល

somewhere   gon-laing naa moo-ay   កន្លែងណាមួយ

son   goan bproh   កូនប្រុស

song   jom-ree-ung   ចម្រៀង

soon   nou bpayl jeut jeut nih   នៅពេលជិត ៗ នេះ

sore   cheu   ឈឺ

sorry *(apology)*   soam dtoah   សូមទោស

   (regret)   s'dai   ស្តាយ

   I am very sorry   k'nyom s'dai nah   ខ្ញុំស្តាយណាស់

   I am sorry to hear that . . .   k'nyom soam joo-ay s'dai
taa   ខ្ញុំសូមជួយស្តាយថា ...

so that   darm-bay   ដើម្បី

sound (n)   soa som-layng   សូរសម្លេង

soup   sOOp; som-lor dteuk   ស៊ុប; សម្លទឹក

   rice soup   bor-bor   បបរ

sour   joo   ជូរ

south   kaang t'boang   ខាងត្បូង

Southeast Asia   aa-see aa-k'nay   អាស៊ីអគ្នេយ៍

sow (v)   saap; saap bproo-ah   សាប; សាបព្រោះ

   sow rice   saap s'rou   សាបស្រូវ

spark plug   boo-see   ប៊ូស៊ី

speak   ni-yee-ay   និយាយ

special   bpi-sayh   ពិសេស

speed   l'beu-un   ល្បឿន

spell (v)   sor-say; bpra-gorp   សរសេរ; ប្រកប

spend   jom-nai; brar; jai   ចំណាយ; ប្រើ; ចាយ

spicy *(food)*   heul   ហឹរ

spider   bpeeng bpee-ung   ពីងពាង

spill   gom-bpOOp   កំពប់

spit   s'doh   ស្ដោះ

spoon   s'laap bpree-a   ស្លាបព្រា

sport   gay-laa   កីឡា

spring *(metal)*   laan   ទ្យាន

spring onion   darm k'teum   ដើមខ្ទឹម

square   jato-rayng gaing s'mar   ចតុរង្សកែងស្មើ

   10 square meters   dop mait gror-laa   ១០ ម៉ែត្រក្រឡា

squeeze   gee-up   គាប

squid   dtray-meuk   ត្រីមឹក

stain   s'naam bpra-luk   ស្នាមប្រឡាក់

stairs   gum joo-un-dar   កាជណ្ដើរ

   downstairs   joa-un graom   ជាន់ក្រោម

   upstairs   joa-un ler; ler lou   ជាន់លើ; លើទ្យៅ

stake *(post)*   bong-goal   បង្គោល

stamp (n)   dtaim   តែមប្រ៉ៃ

stamp (v)   bpra-tup dtraa   ប្រថាប់ត្រា

stand (v)   chor   ឈរ

   stand up   chor larng   ឈរឡើង

standard of living   gum-reut jee-wee-a pee-up   កំរិតជីវិភាព

star *(movie, planet)*   daa-raa; p'gai   តារា; ផ្កាយ

stare som-leung merl សម្លឹងមើល

start *(begin)* jup p'darm ចាប់ផ្ដើម

   start a motor boñ-cheh maa-seen បញ្ចេះម៉ាស៊ីន

   starting from dtung bpee តាំងពី

starve *(be starving)* ot bai; ot klee-un អត់បាយ; អត់ឃ្លាន

state *(condition)* pee-up ភាព

   (territory) roa-ut រដ្ឋ

station s'taa-nee; jom-nort ស្ថានីយ; ចំណត

   gas station s'taa-nee bprayng sung ស្ថានីយប្រេងសាំង

   police station s'taa-nee dtom-roo-ut ស្ថានីយតម្រួត

   radio station s'taa-nee wit-yOO p'sai som-layng

ស្ថានីយវិទ្យុផ្សាយសម្លេង

   railway station s'taa-nee a-ya-s'mai roo-ut

ស្ថានីយអយស្ម័យរថ

statistics steut-dte ស្ថិតិ

statue roop som-naak រូបសំណាក

stay *(at hotel)* s'nuk nou; som-raak ស្នាក់នៅ; សម្រាក

steal loo-ich លួច

steam *(n)* jom-hai ចំហាយ

steam *(v)* jom-hoy ចំហុយ

   steamed rice bai jom-hoy បាយចំហុយ

steamer *(ship)* ga-bul dot t'yoong កប៉ាល់ដុតឧ្យួង

steel daik taip ដែកថែប

step *(n)* jOOm-hee-un ជំហាន

step *(v)* chee-un ឈាន

stick (n)   dom-borng   ដំបង

stick (v)   joa-up jeut; sa-eut joa-up   ជាប់ចិត្ត; ស្ទិតជាប់

sticky   sa-eut   ស្ទិត

   sticky rice   bai dom-narp   បាយដំណើប

still (adv)   nou . . . nou lar-ee   នៅ ... នៅឡើយ

stingy   gom-nuñ   កំណាញ់

stink (v)   gleun aa-grok; sa-oy   ក្លិនអាក្រក់; ស្អុយ

stir   goa   កូរ

stockings   s'raom jerng nee-long   ស្រោមជើងនីឡុង

stomach   bpoo-ah   ពោះ

stomachache   cheu bpoo-ah   ឈឺពោះ

stone   t'mor   ថ្ម

   precious stone   t'boang   ត្បូង

stop (v)   chOOp   ឈប់

   cause to stop   boñ-chOOp   បញ្ឈប់

store *(shop)*   haang   ហាង

storm *(rain)*   bp'yOOh plee-ung   ព្យុះភ្លៀង

   (wind)   k'yol bp'yOOh   ខ្យល់ព្យុះ

story   reu-ung   រឿង

stove   jerng graan   ជើងក្រាន

straight   dtrong   ត្រង់

   go straight on   dtou dtrong ra-hoat   ទៅត្រង់រហូត

strange   bplaik; jom-laik   ប្លែក; ចំឡែក

straw *(drinking)*   bom-bpoo-ung beut   បំពង់បីត

   (rice)   jom-barng   ចំបើង

stream oa អូរ

street wi-tay; plou វិថី; ផ្លូវ

strength gom-lung កម្លាំង

strike (n) *(labor)* goat-da-gum កូដកម្ម

strike (v) *(hit)* wee-ay វាយ

   (labor) t'wer goat-da-gum ធ្វើកូដកម្ម

string k'sai ខ្សែ

stroll (v) dar layng ដើរលេង

strong klung ខ្លាំង

structure (n) kroang គ្រោង

struggle (v) dtor soo តស៊ូ

student goan seuh; ni-seut កូនសិស្ស; និស្សិត

study (v) ree-un រៀន

Stung Treng steung dtraing ស្ទឹងត្រែង

stupid klao; chaot l'ngoo-ung; pler ខ្លៅ; ឆោតល្ងង់; ភ្លើ

style baip; moat បែប; ម៉ូដ

subject *(of study)* mOOk wi-jee-a មុខវិជ្ជា

suburbs jee-ay grong ជាយក្រុង

succeed mee-un joak jay; som-raych មានជោគជ័យ; សម្រេច

success joak-jay ជោគជ័យ

such (as) doach jee-a ដូចជា

suddenly s'rup dtai; plee-um nOOh ស្រាប់តែ; ភ្លាមនោះ

sugar s'gor ស្ករ

sugar cane om-bpou អំពៅ

sugar-palm tree darm t'naot ដើមត្នោត

suggest p'dol yoa-bol ផ្ដល់យោបល់

suicide *(commit)* som-lup kloo-un aing សម្លាប់ខ្លួនឯង

suit *(of clothes)* kao ao ខោអាវ

suitable som-rOOm សមរម្យ

suitcase wah-lee(h); heup kao ao រ៉ាលីស; ហិបខោអាវ

summer ra-dou g'dao រដូវក្ដៅ

sun aa-dteut អាទិត្យ

Sunday t'ngai aa-dteut ថ្ងៃអាទិត្យ

sunny mee-un t'ngai; jeuñ t'ngai មានថ្ងៃ; ចេញថ្ងៃ

sunrise t'ngai ray-ah ថ្ងៃរះ

sunset t'ngai leuch ថ្ងៃលិច

sunshine bpoo-un-leu t'ngai ពន្លឺថ្ងៃ

superstitious jOOm-neu-a koh goo-un-lorng ជំនឿខុសកន្លង

supervise dtroo-ut merl ត្រួតមើល

supervisor nay-uk dtroo-ut merl អ្នកត្រួតមើល

suppose s'maan ស្មាន

supposed (to) dtrou dtai ត្រូវតែ

suppress haam bpraam ហាមប្រាម

sure *(know for sure)* deung jay-uk ដឹងជាក់

  for sure jee-a bpraa-got ជាប្រាកដ

surely *(probably)* bpraa-got jee-a . . . meun kaan ប្រាកដជា ... មិនខាន

surface p'dtay-ee ផ្ទៃ

surname nee-um dtra-goal នាមត្រកូល

surprised p'nyay-uk ភ្ញាក់

surrender (v) joh juñ; joh joal ចុះចាញ់; ចុះចូល

suspect (v) moo-un-dteul song-sai មន្ទិលសង្ស័យ

Svay Rieng swai ree-ung ស្វាយរៀង

swallow layp លេប

swamp wee-ul poo-uk l'bop វាលភក់ល្បប់

swear s'bot ស្បថ

sweat (n) n'yerh ញើស

sweat (v) baik n'yerh បែកញើស

sweep baoh បោស

sweet *(in manner)* dtoo-un ploo-un ទន់ភ្លន់
   (taste) pa-aim ផ្អែម

sweets *(dessert)* bong-aim បង្អែម

swell harm ហើម

swim hail dteuk ហែលទឹក

swimming pool aang hail dteuk អាងហែលទឹក

swimsuit kao ao hail dteuk ខោអាវហែលទឹក

swollen harm ហើម

sword dao ដាវ

symbol kreu-ung som-goa-ul គ្រឿងសំគាល់

sympathize (with) mee-un baa-saat jeut (neung)
   មានប្រាសាទចិត្ត (នឹង)

syphilis roak swai រោគស្វាយ

system ra-borp; ra-bee-up របប; របៀប

T

table　dto　តុ

tablecloth　gom-raal dto　កម្រាលតុ

tail　gon-dtoo-ee　កន្ទុយ

tailor　jee-ung gut day　ជាងកាត់ដេរ

　tailor's shop　haang gut day　ហាងកាត់ដេរ

take *(things)*　yoak　យក

　(something somewhere)　yoak . . . dtou . . .　យក . . . ទៅ
　. . .

take *(medicine)*　peuk t'num; layp t'num　ផឹកថ្នាំ; លេបថ្នាំ

　(someone)　noa-um; joon　នាំ; ជូន

　(someone somewhere)　noa-um . . . dtou . . .; joon . . . dtou
　. . . នាំ...ទៅ...; ជូន...ទៅ...

take off *(clothes)*　doh kao ao　ដោះខោអាវ

Takéo　dtaa-gai-o　តាកែវ

talk (v)　ni-yee-ay　និយាយ

talks (n) *(negotiations)*　gaa jor-jaa　ការចរចា

tall　k'bpoo-ah　ខ្ពស់

tame　sung　សាំង

tank　tOOng　ធុង

　gasoline tank　tOOng sung　ធុងសាំង

　military tank　roo-ut-groh　រថក្រោះ

　water tank　tOOng dteuk　ធុងទឹក

tape *(cellophane)* k'sai joa-a s'eut ខ្សែជ័រស្អិត
   (measuring) k'sai rorng-woa-ah ខ្សែរង្វាស់
   (recording) k'sai ut tort som-layng ខ្សែអាត់ថតសំ
ឡេង

tape recorder maa-seen tort som-layng ម៉ាស៊ីនថត
សំឡេង

taste (n) roo-ah jee-ut រសជាតិ

taste (v) ploo-uk ភ្លក់
   does it taste good? ch'nguñ dtay? ឆ្ងាញ់ទេ ?

tasteless k'mee-un jee-ut គ្មានជាតិ

tasty ch'nguñ; ch'ngoo-ee ch'nguñ ឆ្ងាញ់; ឈ្ងុយឆ្ងាញ់

tax (n) bpoo-un ពន្ធ
   pay tax bong bpoo-un បង់ពន្ធ

taxi dtuk-see តាក់ស៊ី

tea dtai; dteuk dtai តែ; ទឹកតែ

teach bong-ree-un បង្រៀន

teacher kroo bong-ree-un គ្រូបង្រៀន

teak cher mai suk ឈើម៉ៃសាក់

team *(group)* grom ក្រុម

teapot bpun dtai ប៉ាន់តែ

tear (v) haik ហែក
   torn ra-haik រហែក

teardrop dteuk p'nairk ទឹកភ្នែក

tease jom-ork layng ចំអកលេង

teeth t'mayñ ធ្មេញ

telegram   dtay-lay graam; dtoo-ra-layk   តេឡេក្រាម; ទូរលេខ

telephone (n)   dtoo-ra-sup   ទូរស័ព្ទ

telephone (v)   dtoo-ra-sup dtou . . .   ទូរស័ព្ទទៅ...
  to talk on the telephone   ni-yee-ay dtaam dtoo-ra-sup   និយាយតាមទូរស័ព្ទ

telephone number   layk dtoo-ra-sup   លេខទូរស័ព្ទ

telescope   gai-o yeut   កែវយឺត

television   dtoo-ra-dtoa-a   ទូរទស្សន៍

tell   ni-yee-ay bprup   និយាយប្រាប់
  tell a story   ni-dtee-un reu-ung   និទានរឿង

temperature   gom-dao; gom-reut gom-dao   កំដៅ; កម្រិតកំដៅ

temple   woa-ut   វត្ត

temporary   bon-doh aa-son   បណ្ដោះអាសន្ន

ten   dop   ដប់

ten thousand   meun   ម៉ឺន

tent   dtong   តង់

termite   gon-dee-a   កណ្ដៀរ

terrorism   pay-ra-wee-a-gum   ភេរវកម្ម

terrorist   pay-ra-wee-a-joo-un   ភេរវជន

test *(examination)*   gaa bpra-lorng   ការប្រឡង
  take a test   bpra-lorng   ប្រឡង

test (v)   bpi-saoch   ពិសោធ

textile   dtom-baañ   តម្បាញ

textile mill roang juk dtom-baañ រោងចក្រតម្បាញ

Thai tai ថៃ

Thailand bpra-dtayh tai ប្រទេសថៃ

than jee-ung ជាង

   more than j'ram jee-ung ច្រើនជាង

thank *(thank you)* or-gOOn អរគុណ

that nOOh នោះ

theater roang l'kaon រោងល្ខោន

their(s) ra-boh gay របស់គេ

then *(after that)* roo-ich moak; grao-ee moak; រួចមក;
ក្រោយមក; bon-dtoa-up moak បន្ទាប់មក

   (at that time) bpayl nOOh ពេលនោះ

   (therefore) doach-nih; uñ-jeung ដូច្នេះ; អញ្ចឹង

theory dtreuh-s'day ទ្រឹស្តី

there ai nOOh ឯនោះ

therefore dao-ee hait nih ដោយហេតុនេះ

thermometer kreu-ung stoo-ung gom-dao គ្រឿងស្ទួង
កំដៅ

these dtay-ung nih ទាំងនេះ`

they gay គេ

thick grah ក្រាស់

thief jao ចោរ

thin *(people)* s'gorm ស្គម

   (things) s'darng ស្ដើង

thing(s) ra-boh របស់

think   geut; yoo-ul   គិត; យល់

   I think so   k'nyom yoo-ul yaang nih aing   ខ្ញុំយល់យ៉ាង
   នេះឯង

   I don't think so   k'nyom meun yoo-ul yaang nih dtay
   ខ្ញុំមិនយល់យ៉ាងនេះទេ

third *(place)*   dtee bay   ទីបី

   (one-third)   moo-ay pee-uk bay   មួយភាគបី

thirsty   s'rayk dteuk   ស្រេកទឹក

thirty   saam seup   សាមសិប

this   nih   នេះ

   this way; like this   yaang nih   យ៉ាងនេះ

thorn   bon-laa   បន្លា

those   dtay-ung nOOh   ទាំងនោះ

thought (n)   gOOm-neut   គំនិត

thousand   bpoa-un   ពាន់

   hundred thousand   sain   សែន

   ten thousand   meun   ម៉ឺន

thread (n)   sor-sai   សសៃ

three   bay   បី

   three or four   bay boo-un   បីបួន

throat   bom-bpoo-ung gor   បំពង់ក

   have a sore throat   ra-lee-uk bom-bpoo-ung gor
   រលាកបំពង់ក

through   dtaam   តាម

   pass through . . .   ch'long gut dtaam . . .   ឆ្លងកាត់តាម . . .

throw (v) boh; jaol ព្រោះ; ចោល

   throw away boh jaol ព្រោះចោល

thumb may dai មេដៃ

thunder p'gor ផ្គរ

Thursday t'ngai bpra-hoa-ah ថ្ងៃព្រហស្បតិ៍

ticket som-bot សំបុត្រ

tidy ree-up roy; sa-aat baat រៀបរយ; ស្អាតបាត

tie (v) jorng; jorng p'joa-up ចង; ចងភ្ជាប់

ties (n) *(links)* jom-norng ចំណង

   (neck)tie gra-wut ក្រវ៉ាត់

tiger klaa ខ្លា

tight *(clothes)* dteung តឹង

time bpayl; way-lee-a; gaal ពេល; វេលា; កាល

   a long time yoo យូរ

   on time dtoa-un maong ទាន់ម៉ោង

   what time is it? maong bpon-maan hai? ម៉ោងប៉ុន្មាន
ហើយ ?

timetable dtaa-raang bpayl way-lee-a តារាងពេលវេលា

tin *(can)* gom-bpong som-na bpaa-hung
កំប៉ុងសំណប៉ាហាំង

   (metal) som-na bpaa-hung សំណប៉ាហាំង

tiny dtoach dtaach; la-eut តូចតាច; ល្អិត

tip *(end)* jong ចុង

tire *(rubber)* gao soo កៅស៊ូ

tired *(exhausted)* oh gom-lung; neu-ay hot អស់កម្លាំង;

នឿយហត់

tired of *(bored)* neu-ay nai; tOOñ dtroa-un   នឿយណាយ;
ធុញទ្រាន់

to *(in order to)* darm-bay   ដើម្បី
 (toward) dol   ដល់

tobacco t'num joo-uk   ថ្នាំជក់

today t'ngai nih   ថ្ងៃនេះ

together ji-moo-ay k'nee-a   ជាមួយគ្នា
 all together dtay-ung oh k'nee-a   ទាំងអស់គ្នា

toilet bong-goo-un   បង្គន់
 toilet paper gra-daah som-rup bong-goo-un
   ក្រដាសសំរាប់បង្គន់

tomato bpayng boh   ប៉េងប៉ោះ

tomorrow sa-aik   ស្អែក
 the day after tomorrow kaan sa-aik   ខានស្អែក

tongue on-daat   អណ្ដាត

tonight yOOp nih   យប់នេះ

Tonlé Sap *(Sap River)* dtoo-un-lay saap   ទន្លេសាប

too dai; porng   ដែរ, ផង
 (too much) …j'ram bpayk   … ច្រើនពេក
 me too k'nyom dai   ខ្ញុំដែរ

tool bpra-dup bpra-daa   ប្រដាប់ប្រដា

tooth t'mayñ   ធ្មេញ

toothache cheu t'mayñ   ឈឺធ្មេញ

toothbrush j'raah doh t'mayñ   ច្រាសដុសធ្មេញ

toothpaste m'sao doh t'mayñ ម្សៅដុះធ្មេញ

toothpick cher juk t'mayñ ឈើចាក់ធ្មេញ

top *(cover, lid)* gOOm-rorp; krorp គំរប, គ្រប

 (on top) kaang ler ខាងលើ

 (summit) gom-bpool កំពូល

torn dtoo-uk; ra-haik ទុក; រហែក

tortoise un-dark អណ្ដើក

torture *(n)* dtee-a-rOOn-na-gum ទារុណកម្ម

total *(number)* jom-noo-un saa-rop ចំនួនសារុប

touch *(v)* bpah; bpoa-ul ប៉ះ; ពាល់

tough *(as of meat)* s'weut ស្វិត

tour guide nay-uk noa-um dom-nar dtay-sa-jor; អ្នកនាំ
ដំណើរទេសចរណ៍; nay-uk mayk-gOO-dtayh
អ្នកមគ្គុទ្ទេសក៍

tourism dtay-sa-jor ទេសចរណ៍

tourist nay-uk dtay-sa-jor អ្នកទេសចរណ៍

towel gon-saing កន្សែង

tower bporm ប៉ម

town dtee grong; p'saa ទីក្រុង; ផ្សារ

toy kreu-ung layng គ្រឿងលេង

track *(railway)* plou daik; plou ra-dtayh plerng ផ្លូវ
ដែក, ផ្លូវរទេះភ្លើង

tractor dtruk-dtoa-a ត្រាក់ទ័រ

trade *(v)* jOOm-noo-uñ ជំនួញ

traffic ja-raa-jor ចរាចរ

trail *(path)* plou lum ផ្លូវលំ

train (n) ra-dtayh plerng រទេះភ្លើង

train (v) *(for something)* hut ហាត់

   (someone) bong-hut បង្ហាត់

traitor joo-un g'bot jee-ut ជនក្បត់ជាតិ

translate bork-bprai បកប្រែ

translation gaa bork bprai ការបកប្រែ

translator nay-uk bork bprai អ្នកបកប្រែភាសា

trap (n) on-dtay-uk អន្ទាក់

trap (v) dtay-uk ទាក់

trash *(rubbish)* som-nol; som-raam សំណល់; សម្រាម

travel (n) gaa t'wer dom-nar ការធ្វើដំណើរ

travel (v) t'wer dom-nar ធ្វើដំណើរ

   (for pleasure) t'wer dom-nar gom-saan layng ធ្វើ
ដំណើរកំសាន្តលេង

traveler nay-uk dom-nar អ្នកដំណើរ

tray taah ថាស

tree darm cher ដើមឈើ

triangle dtray gaon ត្រីកោណ

trick (n) gol; gol OO-bai; l'beuch កល; កលឧបាយ; ល្បិច

trip *(journey)* gaa t'wer dom-nar ការធ្វើដំណើរ

trip (v) dtay-uk doo-ul ទាក់ដួល

trouble *(difficulty)* gaa bpi-baak ការពិបាក

trousers kao ខោ

truck laan deuk dtOOm-neuñ ឡានដឹកទំនិញ

true bpeut; bpeut maim ពិត; ពិតមែន

trust (v) (jeu-a) dtOOk jeut (ជឿ)ទុកចិត្ត

truth gaa bpeut ការពិត

try *(persevere)* kom bp'yee-a yee-um ខំព្យាយាម

  try out; try on lor merl; l'borng merl; saak merl
  មើល; ល្បងមើល; សាកមើល

tube bom-bpoo-ung បំពង់

tuberculosis roak ra-bayng រោគរបេង

Tuesday t'ngai ong-gee-a ថ្ងៃអង្គារ

turn (v) *(left or right)* bot បត់

  (spin) bong-weul បង្វិល

turn on *(a switch)* bark បើក

turn off *(a switch)* beut បិទ

twelve dop bpee; bpee don-dop ដប់ពីរ; ពីរដណ្ដប់

twenty m'pay ម្ភៃ

twice bpee dorng ពីរដង

twins ploo-ah ភ្លោះ

twist (v) moo-ul មូល

two bpee ពីរ

type (n) baip; bpra-payt បែប; ប្រភេទ

type (v) wee-ay duk-dtee-loa វាយដាក់ទិឡូ

typewriter duk-dtee-loa; maa-seen ong-goo-lee layk
  ដាក់ទិឡូ; ម៉ាស៊ីនអង្គុលីលេខ

typhoid fever grOOn son-tOOm គ្រុនសន្ធំ

typist nay-uk wee-ay duk-dtee-loa អ្នកវាយដាក់ទិឡូ

U

ugly aa-grok merl; meun sa-aat   អាក្រក់មើល; មិនស្អាត

umbrella chut   ឆត្រ

unbutton doh lay-ew   ដោះឡេវ

uncle mee-a; σa-bpOOk mee-a   មា; ឪពុកមា

unconditional ot jom-norng   ឥតចំណង

under graom; kaang graom   ក្រោម; ខាងក្រោម

underpants kao dtra-noa-up; kao k'nong   ខោទ្រនាប់; ខោក្នុង

undershirt ao dtra-noa-up; ao k'nong   អាវទ្រនាប់; អាវក្នុង

understand yoo-ul   យល់

I do not understand k'nyom meun yoo-ul dtay
ខ្ញុំមិនយល់ទេ

misunderstand yoo-ul j'ra-lum; yoo-ul koh   យល់ច្រឡំ; យល់ខុស

underwear kao ao dtra-noa-up; kao ao k'nong   ខោអាវទ្រនាប់; ខោអាវក្នុង

undress doh kao ao   ដោះខោអាវ

unemployed k'mee-un gaa t'wer   គ្មានការធ្វើ

unhappy meun sop-bai   មិនសប្បាយ

uniform aik son-taan   ឯកសណ្ឋាន

unite boñ-joal k'nee-a; roo-up roo-um k'nee-a   បញ្ជូលគ្នា; រួបរួមគ្នា

United Nations ong-gaa sa-haa bpra-jee-a jee-ut
អង្គការសហប្រជាជាតិ

United States sa-haa roa-ut aa-may-rik សហរដ្ឋអាមេរិក

university saa-gol wit-yee-a-lai សាកលវិទ្យាល័យ

unlock bark sao បើកសោ

unlucky k'mee-un som-naang គ្មានសំណាង

unmarried nou lew នៅលីវ

unofficial grao plou gaa ក្រៅផ្លូវការ

untie doh jeuñ ដោះចេញ

until dtoa-ul tai; dol; ra-hoat dol ទាល់តែ; ដល់;
រហូតដល់

  Go straight on until you see . . . dar dtrong dtou mOOk ra-
  hoat dol kerñ . . . ដើរត្រង់ទៅមុខរហូតដល់ឃើញ ...

  I'll wait until he arrives k'nyom jum dtoa-ul tai goa-ut
  moak dol ខ្ញុំចាំទាល់តែគាត់មកដល់

up *(get up, go up, rise)* larng ឡើង

Upper Khmer *(Cambodian hill tribes)* k'mai ler ខ្មែរលើ

upstairs kaang ler lou; joa-un kaang ler ខាងលើឡៅ;
ជាន់ខាងលើ

urgent bon-dtoa-un បន្ទាន់

urinate noam នោម

urine dteuk noam ទឹកនោម

us yerng; yerng k'nyom យើង; យើងខ្ញុំ

use (v) brar ប្រើ

used to *(accustomed to)* t'loa-up neung ធ្លាប់នឹង

(formerly...) t'loa-up ធ្លាប់

useful mee-un bpra-yaoch មានប្រយោជន៍

useless k'mee-un bpra-yaoch គ្មានប្រយោជន៍

usually jee-a toa-um-a-daa ជាធម្មតា

V

vacant dtOOm-nay ទំនេរ

vacation wi-sa-ma-gaal វិស្សមកាល

vaccinate juk t'num bong-gaa roak ចាក់ថ្នាំបង្ការរោគ

vagina yoa-nee យោនិ

valley j'ra-lorng p'nOOm ជ្រលងភ្នំ

valuable mee-un dtom-lai; t'lai t'laa មានតម្លៃ; ថ្លៃថ្លា

value dtom-lai តម្លៃ

various p'sayng p'sayng ផ្សេង ៗ

vase toa ថូ

vegetable bon-lai បន្លែ

vehicle yee-un jOOm-nih យានជំនិះ

vendor nay-uk loo-uk អ្នកលក់

venereal disease roak dayk neung s'ray; gaam-ma-roak រោគដេកនឹងស្រី; កាមរោគ

verb gay-ri-yaa កិរិយា

very nah; grai-lairng ណាស់; ក្រៃលែង

not very... meun sou... មិនសូវ ...

vet bpa-so-bpairt បសុពេទ្យ

via dtaam តាម

vicinity *(in the vicinity)* nou jeut kaang នៅជិតខាង

Vietnam wee-ut naam · វៀតណាម

view *(scenic)* dtay-sa-pee-up ទេសភាព

village poom ភូមិ

villager nay-uk poom អ្នកភូមិ

vinegar dteuk k'meh ទឹកខ្មេះ

virtue gOOn-na-toa-a គុណធម៌

visa dteut-taa-gaa ទិដ្ឋាការ

visit (v) dtou layng ទៅលេង

visitor p'nyee-o ភ្ញៀវ

vitamin wee-dtaa-min វីតាមីន

voice som-layng សម្លេង

volunteer (v) s'muk jeut ស្ម័គ្រចិត្ត

vomit (v) jong-ao; ga-oo-ut ចង្អោរ; ក្អួត

vote (v) boh ch'naot បោះឆ្នោត

vowel s'ra ស្រៈ

W

wage(s) bpruk ch'noo-ul; bpruk kai ប្រាក់ឈ្នួល; ប្រាក់ខែ

waist jong-geh ចង្កេះ

wait jum; roo-ung jum ចាំ; រង់ចាំ

wait a moment   jum moo-ay plairt   ចាំមួយភ្លែត

waiter, waitress   nay-uk bom-rar dto   អ្នកបំរើតុ

wake up   p'nyay-uk   ភ្ញាក់

wake someone up   dah   ដាស់

walk   dar   ដើរ

wall   joo-uñ-jay-ung   ជញ្ជាំង

wallet   gaa-boap bpruk   កាបូបប្រាក់

want   jong; jong baan   ចង់; ចង់បាន

war   jom-bung; song-kree-um   ចំបាំង; សង្គ្រាម

civil war   song-kree-um see-wil   សង្គ្រាមស៊ីវិល

wardrobe   dtoo kao-ao   ទូខោអាវ

warehouse   klay-ung   ឃ្លាំង

warm   g'dao   ក្ដៅ

(affectionate)   gok g'dao   កក់ក្ដៅ

wash   doh lee-ung   ដុសលាង

wash and iron   baok OOt   បោកអ៊ុត

wash clothes   doh lee-ung kao ao   ដុសលាងខោអាវ

wash hair   lee-ung sok; gok sok   លាងសក់; កក់សក់

washerman/woman   nay-uk baok OOt   អ្នកបោកអ៊ុត

waste (v)   k'jay-ah k'jee-ay   ខ្ជះខ្ជាយ

waste money   k'jay-ah k'jee-ay loo-ee guk
ខ្ជះខ្ជាយលុយកាក់

waste time   k'jay-ah k'jee-ay bpayl way-lee-a   ខ្ជះខ្ជាយ
ពេលវេលា

watch (n)   nee-a-li-gaa dai   នាឡិកាដៃ

watch (v)   merl   មើល

   watch out!   bpra-yut   ប្រយ័ត្ន .

watchman   nay-uk yee-um   អ្នកយាម

water (n)   dteuk   ទឹក

   boiled water   dteuk cha'eun   ទឹកឆ្អិន

   cold water   dteuk dtra-jay-uk   ទឹកត្រជាក់

   distilled water   dteuk jum-hoy.   ទឹកចំហុយ

   drinking water   dteuk peuk   ទឹកផឹក

   fresh water   dteuk saap   ទឹកសាប

   hot water   dteuk g'dao   ទឹកក្ដៅ

   iced water   dteuk gork   ទឹកកក

   rain water   dteuk plee-ung   ទឹកភ្លៀង

   salt water   dteuk um-beul   ទឹកអំបិល

   well water   dteuk un-doang   ទឹកអណ្ដូង

water (v)   s'raoch dteuk   ស្រោចទឹក

water buffalo   gra-bay   ក្របី

water melon   oa-leuk   ឪឡឹក

waterfall   dteuk t'lay-uk; dteuk j'roo-ah   ទឹកធ្លាក់; ទឹកជ្រោះ

wave (n) *(in the sea)*   ra-lork   រលក

wave (v) *(something)*   gra-wee   គ្រវី

   (the hand)   bok dai   បក់ដៃ

way *(method, means)*   wi-tee; ra-bee-up   វិធី; របៀប

   (route, path)   plou   ផ្លូវ

   this way; like this   yaang nih   យ៉ាងនេះ

we yerng យើង

weak *(exhausted)* oh gum-lung bpayk អស់កម្លាំងពេក
   (frail) k'sao-ee; meun klung ខ្សោយ; មិនខ្លាំង

wealthy mee-un មាន

weapon aa-wOOt អាវុធ

wear *(clothes)* slee-uk bpay-uk ស្លៀកពាក់
   (lower garment) slee-uk ស្លៀក
   (upper garment) bpay-uk ពាក់

weather tee-ut aa-gaah ធាតុអាកាស

weave t'baañ ត្បាញ

wed ree-up gaa រៀបការ

wedding aa-bpee-a bpi-bpaa; mong-goo-ul-gaa
   អាពាហ៍ពិពាហ៍; មង្គលការ

Wednesday t'ngai bpOOt ថ្ងៃពុធ

week aa-dteut អាទិត្យ
   last week aa-dteut mOOn អាទិត្យមុន
   next week aa-dteut grao-ee អាទិត្យក្រោយ

weekend jong aa-dteut ចុងអាទិត្យ

weigh t'leung ថ្លឹង
   how much does it weigh? mee-un dtOOm-ngoo-un bpon-
   maan? មានទម្ងន់ប៉ុន្មាន?

weight dtOOm-ngoo-un ទម្ងន់

welcome *(visitors)* swah-gOOm; dtor-dtoo-ul ស្វាគមន៍;
   ទទួល

well *(do something well)* bpeun bpra-sop ប៊ិនប្រសប់

you speak Khmer well   loak ni-yee- ay k'mai la-or

លោកនិយាយខ្មែរល្អ

well *(healthy)* sok-sop-bai សុខសប្បាយ

I don't feel well   k'nyom meun s'roo-ul kloo-un dtay

ខ្ញុំមិនស្រួលខ្លួនទេ

to get well   baan jee-a s'roo-ul larng weuñ

បានជាស្រួលឡើងវិញ

well (n)   (water, oil) on-doang   អណ្ដូង

west   kaang leuch   ខាងលិច

wet   dtor-dteuk; sarm   ទឹក; សើម

what   a-way; ay; sa'ay   អ្វី; អី; ស្អី

what's this   sa-ay nih   ស្អីនេះ

when   bpayl naa   ពេលណា

whenever   bpayl naa   ពេលណា

where   ai-naa *or* ee- naa   ឯណា

which   dail   ដែល

which one?   naa?; moo-ay naa?   ណា? មួយណា?

while *(during)*   k'nong bpayl   ក្នុងពេល

whip (v)   wee-ay   វាយ

whiskey   s'raa wi-skee   ស្រាវិស្គី

whisper   ni-yee-ay k'seup   និយាយខ្សឹប

white   bpoa-a sor   ពណ៌ស

who   nay-uk naa; nor naa   អ្នកណា; នរណា

whole   dtay-ung mool; dtay-ung oh   ទាំងមូល; ទាំងអស់

wholeheartedly   oh bpee jeut bpee t'larm   អស់ពីចិត្តពីថ្លើម

why hait ay ហេតុអ្វី

wide dtoo-lee-ay; tom dtoo-lee-ay ទូលាយ; ធំទូលាយ

wife bpra-bpoo-un ប្រពន្ធ

wild *(savage)* bpray-ee ព្រៃ

will *(shall)* neung នឹង

win ch'nay-ah ឈ្នះ

wind *(breeze)* k'yol ខ្យល់

window bong-oo-ich បង្អួច

wing s'laap ស្លាប

winter ra-dou ra-ngee-a រដូវរងា

wipe joot ជូត

wire loo-ah; k'sai loo-ah   លួស; ខ្សែលួស
   barbed wire k'sai loo-ah bon-laa ខ្សែលួសបន្លា

wish *(desire)* jom-nong; bom-norng ចំណង; បំណង

with neung; ji-moo-ay នឹង; ជាមួយ

withdraw dork yoak jeuñ ដកយកចេញ

without dao-ee k'mee-un ដោយគ្មាន

woman s'ray ស្រី

wonderful oh-jaa អស្ចារ្យ

wood *(forest)* bpray-ee ព្រៃ
   (material) cher ឈើ

word bpee-uk; bpee-uk som-day ពាក្យ; ពាក្យសំដី

work (n) gaa-ngee-a ការងា

   (v) t'wer gaa ធ្វើការ

worker nay-uk t'wer gaa អ្នកធ្វើការ

(laborer)   gum-ma-gaa; gum-ma-gor   កម្មការ; កម្មករ

workshop   roang jee-ung   រោងជាង

world   loak; saa-gol-loak   លោក; សាកលលោក

worm   dong-gou   ដង្កូវ

worry *(be concerned)*   bproo-ay   ព្រួយ

worse   aa-grok jee-ung   អាក្រក់ជាង

wound *(wounded)*   ra-boo-ah   របួស

   seriously wounded   ra-boo-ah t'ngoo-un   របួសធ្ងន់

wrap   k'jop; rOOm   ខ្ចប់; រុំ

wrist   gor dai   កដៃ

wristwatch   nee-a-li-gaa dai   នាឡិកាដៃ

write   sor-say   សរសេរ

writer   nay-uk ni-bpoa-un   អ្នកនិពន្ធ

wrong   koh   ខុស

X

xylophone   ra-nee-ut   រនៀត

Y

year   ch'num   ឆ្នាំ

   last year   ch'num mOOn   ឆ្នាំមុន

new year   ch'num t'may   ឆ្នាំថ្មី

new year's day   t'ngai joal ch'num   ថ្ងៃចូលឆ្នាំ

next year   ch'num grao-ee   ឆ្នាំក្រោយ

yell   s'raik   ស្រែក

yellow   bpoa-a leu-ung   ពណ៌លឿង

yes *(female speaker)*   jaa   ចា៎

  (male speaker)   baat   បាទ

yesterday   m'serl meuñ   ម្សិលមិញ

  the day before yesterday   m'serl moo-ay
  t'ngai   ម្សិលមុយថ្ងៃ

yesterday morning   bpreuk m'serl meñ   ព្រឹកម្សិលមិញ

. . . yet?   . . . reu nou?   . . . ឬនៅ ?

  Has he come yet?   goa-ut moak hai reu nou?   គាត់មក
  ហើយឬនៅ?

  No, not yet   nou   នៅ

  I don't know yet   k'nyom meun dtoa-un deung dtay
  ខ្ញុំមិនទាន់ដឹងទេ

you *(to males)*   loak   លោក

  (to older females)   loak s'ray   លោកស្រី

  (to younger females)   nee-ung s'ray   នាងស្រី

young   k'mayng   ក្មេង

  young people   k'mayng k'mayng   ក្មេងៗ

  younger brother   bpa-oan bproh   ប្អូនប្រុស

  younger sister   bpa-oan s'ray   ប្អូនស្រី

your(s)   ra-boh loak (loak s'ray)   របស់លោក(លោកស្រី)

yourself   kloo-un loak (loak s'ray)   ខ្លួនលោក
(លោកស្រី)

Z

zero   soan   សូន្យ
zipper   k'sai root   ខ្សែរូត
zoo   soo-un sut   សួនសត្វ

CAMBODIAN–ENGLISH

a

a-naa-goo-ut អនាគត future
a-naa-mai អនាម័យ sanitary
a-nOO-saa-wa-ree អនុស្សាវរិយ៍ monument
a-nOO-say-nee aik អនុសេនិៈក captain *(army)*
a-nOOñ-n'yaat អនុញ្ញាត permit (v), allow
a-pay dtoah អភ័យទោស forgive
a-pi-baal អភិបាល administer
a-way អ្វី what; anything
a-yOOt-dta-toa-a អយុត្តិធម៌ injustice
aa អារ saw (v)
aa-dteut អាទិត្យ week; sun
aa-gaah អាកាស air
aa-gaah-sa-yee-un-taan អាកាសយានដ្ឋាន airport
aa-gee-a អាគារ building
aa-graat អាក្រាត naked
aa-grok អាក្រក់ bad
aa-haa អាហារ meal; food
aa-pee-un អាភៀន heroin, opium
aa-sai-ya-taan អាស័យដ្ឋាន address (n)
aa-see aa-k'nay អាស៊ីអគ្នេយ៍ Southeast Asia
aa-son-na-roak អាសន្នរោគ cholera
aa-tree-ut អាធ្រាត្រ midnight

aa-wOOt អាវុធ weapon

aa-yOO អាយុ age

aach ... baan អាច ... បាន may, can

aang (ngoot) dteuk អាង(ងូត)ទឹក bathtub

ai dtee-ut ឯទៀត other

ai naa ឯណា where, anywhere

ai nih ឯនេះ here

ai nOOh ឯនោះ there

ai ... weuñ ឯ ... វិញ as for ...

aik-ga-ree-ich-pee-up ឯករាជភាព independence

aik-ga-saa ឯកសារ document

aik-ga-seut ឯកសិទ្ធិ privilege

aik-son-taan ឯកសណ្ឋាន uniform

aik-uk-kee-a-ree-ich -a-dtoot ឯកអគ្គរាជទូត ambassador

aik-uk-kee-a-roa-ut- ta-dtoot ឯកអគ្គរដ្ឋទូត ambassador

ao អាវ shirt

ao plee-ung អាវភ្លៀង raincoat

ao tom អាវធំ coat

ao-ee ឲ្យ (អោយ) give; let; cause

ao-ee k'jay ឲ្យ (អោយ)ខ្ញី lend

ao-gaah ឱកាស chance, opportunity

ao-sot-s'taan ឱសថស្ថាន pharmacy

aop reut ឱបរិត hug

ay-lou nih ឥឡូវនេះ now

ayd អេដស៍ AIDS

b

baa　ប្រា　bar *(for drinking)*

baa-ray　ប្រារី　cigarette

baan　ប្រាន　get; able *(can)*

baat　ប្រាទ　yes *(male speaker)*

bai　បាយ　food, rice

bai bpreuk　បាយព្រឹក　breakfast

bai dom-narp　បាយដំណើប　sticky rice

bai jom-hoy　បាយចំហុយ　steamed rice

bai t'ngai dtrong　បាយថ្ងៃត្រង់　lunch

　　ot bai　អត់បាយ　starving

bai dtorng　បៃតង　green

baik　បៃក　break (v) *(something)*

baip　បៃប　model, style

bao　ប្រាវ　sack (n)

baoh　ច្រាស　sweep

baok　ច្រាក　cheat (v)

baok OOt　ច្រាកអ៊ុត　wash and iron

bar　បើ　if

bark　បើក　establish; open; switch on; drive

bark sao　បើកសោ　unlock

bay　បី　three

b'day　ប្ដី　husband

bee-a បៀ card *(playing)*
bee-yair បៀរយ៉ែ beer
ber បឺរ butter
beung បឹង lake
beut បិទ close; switch off
bo-raan បុរាណ ancient
boam ប៉ូម pump (v)
boh bpOOm បោះពុម្ព print (v)
boh ch'naot បោះឆ្នោត elect
boh dtraa បោះត្រា seal (v)
bok បុក collide
bok បក់ blow *(wind)*
bok dai បក់ដៃ wave (v) *(the hand)*
bom-bpeuñ បំពេញ fill
bom-bpeuñ jeut បំពេញចិត្ត please, satisfy
bom-bporng បំពង deep fry
bom-nol បំណុល debt
bom-pai បំភ័យ frighten
bom-plaañ បំផ្លាញ ruin, destroy
bom-pot:nou dtee bom-pot នៅទីបំផុត finally
bom-raam បំរាម ban (n), prohibition
bom-rar បំរើ serve
bom-rong បំរុង prepare
bom-rong dtOOk បំរុងទុក reserve (v)
bon បុណ្យ festival, fair; merit *(Buddhist)*

bon k'maoch បុណ្យខ្មោច funeral

bon-dayñ jaol បណ្ដេញចោល expel

bon-doh aa-son បណ្ដោះអាសន្ន temporary

bon-dteuch បន្តិច a little

bon-dteuch bon-dtoa-ich បន្តិចបន្តួច a little

bon-dtoa-un បន្ទាន់ urgent

bon-dtoa-up បន្ទាប់ next

bon-dtoa-ut បន្ទាត់ ruler *(for measuring)*

bon-dtoah បន្ទោស blame (v)

bon-dtOOh បន្ទុះ explosion

bon-dtOOk បន្ទុក load (n)

bon-dtOOp បន្ទប់ room

bon-dtOOp dayk បន្ទប់ដេក bedroom

bon-dtOOp dteuk បន្ទប់ទឹក bathroom

bon-dtOOp dtor-dtoo-ul p'nyee-o បន្ទប់ទទួលភ្ញៀវ living room

bon-dtOOp n'yum bai បន្ទប់ញ៉ាំបាយ dining room

bon-joal dteuk បញ្ចូលទឹក irrigate

bon-lai បន្លែ vegetable

bon-too aa-rom បន្ទរអារម្ម relax

bong t'lai បង់ថ្លៃ pay (v)

bong-aim បង្អែម sweet(s), dessert

bong-gaa បង្ការ prevent

bong-gart បង្កើត establish

bong-goal បង្គោល stake, post

bong-goo-un បង្គន់ toilet

bong-gorng បង្គង prawn, shrimp

bong-gun day បង្កាន់ដៃ receipt

bong-haañ បង្ហាញ show (v)

bong-hai-ee បង្ហើយ finish *(something)*

bong-hut បង្ហាត់ train *(someone)*

bong-kom បង្ខំ force (v)

bong-oo-ich បង្អួច window

bong-ree-un បង្រៀន teach

boñ-cheh maa-seen បញ្ឆេះម៉ាស៊ីន start an engine

boñ-chOOp បញ្ឈប់ cause to stop

boñ-jee-a បញ្ជា order (n) (v)

boñ-joh (dtom-lai) បញ្ចុះ(តម្លៃ) lower (v) (price)

boñ-jop បញ្ចប់ finish *(something)*

boo-ah បួស enter the monkhood

boo-see ប៊ូស៊ី spark plug

boo-un បួន four

bor-boa moa-ut បបូរមាត់ lips

bor-bor បបរ rice gruel

bor-ra-dtayh បរទេស foreign

bor-ri-sut បរិស័ទ company

bor-ri-wayn បរិវេណ area

bork បក peel (v)

bork-bprai បកប្រែ translate

    nay-uk bork-bprai អ្នកបកប្រែ interpreter

borng បង elder sibling

borng bpa-oan បងប្អូន brothers and sisters

borng bproh បងប្រុស elder brother

borng s'ray បងស្រី elder sister

bot បត់ fold; turn

bot o-greut បទឧក្រិដ្ឋ crime

brar ប្រើ use (v)

buk បាក់ break *(a bone)*

buk-say បក្សី bird

bul បាល់ ball

bun-jee បញ្ជី list

bun-naa-lai បណ្ណាល័យ library

bung បាំង hide (v)

buñ បាញ់ fire (v) (a gun)

but បាត់ lose; disappear

bp

bpa-de-sayt បដិសេធ refuse (v)

bpa-de-woa-ut បដិវត្តន៍ revolution

bpa-oan bproh ប្អូនប្រុស younger brother

bpa-oan s'ray ប្អូនស្រី younger sister

bpa-ri-yaa-gaah បរិយាកាស atmosphere

bpa-so-bpairt បសុពេទ្យ vet

bpa-tom seuk-saa បឋមសិក្សា primary education

bpaa-gaa ប៉ាកា pen

bpah ប៉ះ touch (v)

bpairng ពែង cup

bpairt ពែទ្យ doctor

bpairt t'mayñ ពែទ្យធ្មេញ dentist

bpait seup ប៉ែតសិប eighty

bpay-ung ពាំង block (v), obstruct

bpayk ពេក extremely

bpayl ពេល time; when

   bpayl naa? ពេលណា? when?

bpee ពី from; about *(concerning)*

bpee ពីរ two

bpee-uk ពាក្យ word

bpee-ung ពាង jar *(for storing water)*

bpeun bpra-sop ប៊ិនប្រសប់ well *(do something well)*

bpeuñ ពេញ full

bpeuñ jeut ពេញចិត្ត satisfied

bpeut ពិត real, true

bpi-baak ពិបាក difficult

bpi-bproo-ah ពិព្រោះ because

bpi-kroo-ah ពិគ្រោះ consult

bpi-neut ពិនិត្យ inspect, examine

bpi-roo-ah ពិរោះ melodious

bpi-saa ពិសា eat *(polite)*

bpi-saoch ពិសោធន៍ experiment (v), test (v)

bpi-sayh ពិសេស special

bpi-tee ពិធី ceremony

bplaik ប្លែក strange, unusual

bplon ប្លន់ rob

bpoa-dta-mee-un ពត៌មាន information, news

bpoa-a ពណិ៌ color

bpoa-ul ពាល់ touch (v)

bpoa-un ពាន់ thousand

bpon-dtai ប៉ុន្តែ but

bpon-maan ប៉ុន្មាន how much, how many

bpong-seu-mong ប៉ង់សីម៉ង់ bandage (n)

bpook ពូក mattress

bpoo-ah ពោះ stomach

bpoo-ah ពស់ snake

bpoo-gai ពូកែ skilled, good at

bpoo-tao ពូថៅ ax

bpoo-uk ពួក group

bpoo-uk maak ពួកម៉ាក friend

bpoo-un ពន្ធ tax (n)

bpoo-un-leu ពន្លឺ light

bpoo-un-yoo-ul ពន្យល់ explain

bpOOk moa-ut ពុកមាត់ mustache

bpOOt-ta-saa-s'naa ពុទ្ធសាសនា Buddhism

bpor-bpork ពពក cloud

bporm ប៉ម tower

bporng ពង egg

bpra-bpoo-un ប្រពន្ធ wife

bpra-dul ប្រដាល់ boxing

   nay-uk bpra-dul អ្នកប្រដាល់ boxer

bpra-dup bpra-daa ប្រដាប់ប្រដា tool

bpra-dtayh ប្រទេស country

bpra-gaah ប្រកាស announce (v); notice (n)

bpra-gra-de-dtin ប្រក្រតិទិន calendar

bpra-haa jee-weut ប្រហារជីវិត execute *(a criminal)*

bpra-hail ប្រហែល about *(approximately)*; perhaps

bpra-hail k'nee-a ប្រហែលគ្នា similar

bpra-jee-a-joo-un ប្រជាជន people, population

bpra-jOOm ប្រជុំ meeting

bpra-jun ប្រចិណ្ឌ jealous

bpra-lai ប្រឡាយ canal

bpra-leum ព្រលឹម dawn, early morning

bpra-lOOp ព្រលប់ early evening

bpra-lorng ប្រឡង take an exam

bpra-maan ប្រមាណ about *(approximately)*

bpra-moal ប្រមូល gather *(collect)*

bpra-mOOk ប្រមុខ leader

bpra-nung ប្រណាំង race *(competition)*

bpra-n'yup ប្រញាប់ hurry

bpra-op ប្រអប់ box (n)

bpra-payt ប្រភេទ　type, kind
bpra-peh ប្រផេះ　grey
bpra-sar ប្រសើរ　excellent
bpra-seut-ti-pee-up ប្រសិទ្ធិភាព　efficiency
bpra-sop ប្រសព្វ　intersection
bpra-tee-un ប្រធាន　president, chairman
bpra-woa-ut ប្រវត្តិ　background; record
bpra-woa-ut-ta-saah ប្រវត្តិសាស្ត្រ　history
bpra-yaoch ប្រយោជន៍　advantage, benefit
bpra-yoak ប្រយោគ　sentence *(grammar)*
bpra-yOOt ប្រយុទ្ធ　fight (v) *(soldiers)*
bpra-yut ប្រយ័ត្ន　watch out!
bpraach-n'yaa ប្រាជ្ញា　intelligent
bprai ប្រៃ　salty
bprai-sa-nee-ya-bot ប្រៃសណីយបត្រ　postcard
bprai-sa-nee-ya-taan ប្រៃសណីយដ្ឋាន　post office
bpray-ah ព្រះ　God
bpray-ah bpOOt ព្រះពុទ្ធ　Buddha
bpray-ah ree-ich-a-nee ព្រះរាជនី　queen
bpray-ee ព្រៃ　jungle, forest; wild
bprayng ប្រេង　oil
bprayng sung ប្រេងសាំង　petrol, gasoline
bpree-up tee-up ប្រៀបធៀប　compare
bpreuk ព្រឹក　morning; early *(morning)*
bpreul ព្រិល　snow (n)

bproh ប្រុស man; male

bproo-ah ព្រោះ because

bproo-ay ព្រួយ worry, sad, upset

bprOOm ព្រំ rug

bprOOm dain ព្រំដែន border *(frontier)*

bpruk ប្រាក់ money, silver

bpruk bpi-nay ប្រាក់ពិន័យ fine (n)

bpruk ch'noo-ul ប្រាក់ឈ្នួល wage(s)

bpruk kai ប្រាក់ខែ salary

bprum ប្រាំ five

bprum bay ប្រាំបី eight

bpuk បក្ស party *(political)*

bpun dtai ប៉ាន់តែ teapot, kettle

bpuñ-n'ya-haa បញ្ហា problem

bp'yoo-a ព្យួរ hang

bp'yOOh ព្យុះ storm

c

cha-ait ឆែត full *(from eating)*

cha-eung ឆ្អឹង bone

chaa ឆា stir fry

chao ឆៅ raw

ch'bah ច្បាស់ clear

ch'bup ច្បាប់. law

chee-um ឈាម blood

chee-un ឈាន step (v)

cher ឈើ wood *(material)*

cher gooh ឈើគូស match(es)

cher juk t'mayñ ឈើចាក់ធ្មេញ toothpick

cher mai suk ឈើម៉ៃសាក់ teak

cheu ឈឺ ache; ill

cheu bpoo-ah ឈឺពោះ stomachache

cheu g'baal ឈឺក្បាល headache

cheu t'mayñ ឈឺធ្មេញ toothache

ch'gai ឆ្កែ dog

ch'goo-ut ឆ្កួត mad, crazy

ch'laat ឆ្លាត clever

ch'lar-ee ឆ្លើយ answer (v)

ch'lorng gut ឆ្លងកាត់ cross (v)

ch'maa ឆ្មា cat

ch'moo-ah ឈ្មោះ name (n); to be named

ch'moo-ah dtra-goal ឈ្មោះត្រកូល family name

ch'moo-uñ ឈ្មួញ merchant

ch'nay sa-mot ឆ្នេរសមុទ្រ beach

ch'nay-ah ឈ្នះ win

ch'ngai ឆ្ងាយ far

ch'nguñ ឆ្ងាញ់ tasty, delicious

ch'nok ឆ្នុក plug *(for wash basin)*

ch'noo-ul ឈ្នួល rent (v)

ch'num ឆ្នាំ year

ch'num t'may ឆ្នាំថ្មី new year

choang ឈោង reach *(with one's hand)*

chOOp ឈប់ stop, quit

chor ឈរ stand (v)

chup ឆាប់ fast

chut ឆ័ត្រ umbrella

ch'wayng ឆ្វេង left *(side)*

d

daa-raa ដារា star

dah ដាស់ wake someone up

dai ដែរ also

dai ដៃ arm, hand

daik ដែក iron, steel

daik goal ដែកគោល nail (n)

daik kreep ដែកគ្រីប jack *(for lifting)*

dail ដែល ever *(to have ever done something);* which

dao ដាវ sword

dao-ee ដោយ by

dar ដើរ walk

dar layng ដើរលេង go for a walk, stroll

darm cher ដើមឈើ tree

darm-bay neung ដើម្បីនឹង in order to

day ដី ground, land

day ដេរ sew

dayk ដេក sleep (v)

dayk loo-uk ដេកលក់ fall asleep

dayñ ដេញ chase

dee-ul ដៀល insult (v)

deuk noa-um ដឹកនាំ guide, lead (v)

deung ដឹង know *(information)*

deung gOOn ដឹងគុណ grateful

doa-ich ដូច as, like

doan jee ដូនជី nun

doang ដូង coconut

doh jeuñ ដោះចេញ untie

doh kao ao ដោះខោអាវ undress

doh lairng ដោះលែង release

doh joot ដុសជូត scrub

doh lee-ung ដុសលាង wash

dol ដល់ arrive, reach

dom ដំ pound (v)

dom ដុំ loaf of bread; piece

dom-bao ma-haa-reek ដំបៅមហារីក cancer

dom-boal ដំបូល roof

dom-borng ដំបង stick (n)

dom-larng ដំឡើង increase (v)

dom-loang ដំឡូង potato

dom-nar ដំណើរ journey

dom-neung ដំណឹង information, news

dom-num ដំណាំ crops

dom-ray ដំរី elephant

dong-goa ដង្កូវ worm

dong-hul (uk-gee-sa-nee) ដង្ហាល(អគ្គីសនី) (electric) fan

doo-ul ដួល fall over

dop ដប់ ten

dor-dail ដដែល identical

dork ដក pull out, withdraw

dorng ដង handle

dorng-harm ដង្ហើម breath

dorp ដប bottle

dot ដុត burn (v); bake *(in an oven)*

dot sop ដុតសព cremate

duk ដាក់ put; install; lay down

duk-dtee-loa ដាក់ទីឡ្យ typewriter

dul ដាល់ punch (v)

dum ដាំ boil (v); plant

dt

dta-dteum ទទឹម ruby

dtaam តាម according to; along; via

dtaam dtai . . . តាមតែ . . . it's up to . . .

dtai តែ but; only

dtai តែ tea (plant)

dtaim តែមប្រិ៍ stamp

dtaing dtung តែងតាំង appoint

dtay ទេ question word; no, not

dtay-ah ទះ slap (v)

dtay-sa-jor ទេសចរណ៍ tourism

dtay-sa-pee-up ទេសភាព view *(scenic view)*

dtay-uk ទាក់ trap (v)

dtay-uk doo-ul ទាក់ដួល trip, fall (v)

dtay-uk dtorng ទាក់ទង get in touch with

dtay-ung ទាំង together with, including

dtay-ung bpee ទាំងពីរ both

dtay-ung oh ទាំងអស់ all

dtee bpreuk-saa ទីប្រឹក្សា advisor

dtee grong ទីក្រុង city

dtee lOOm-nou ទីលំនៅ address (n)

dtee bpaa-chaa ទីប៉ាឆា cemetery

dtee-a-hee-un ទាហាន soldier

dtee-un ទៀន candle
dtee-ung dtrong ទៀងត្រង់ honest
dtee-uñ ទាញ pull (v)
dtee-up ទាប short *(in height)*
dtee-ut ទៀត again, more
   m'dorng dtee-ut ម្ដងទៀត again, another . . .
dterh dtoa-ul ទើសទាល់ embarrassed
dteuk ទឹក water
dteuk bpOOh ទឹកពុះ boiled water
dteuk cha'eun ទឹកឆ្អិន boiled water
dteuk doh ទឹកដោះ milk
dteuk dt'ray ទឹកត្រី fish sauce
dteuk dtai ទឹកតែ tea
dteuk gork ទឹកកក ice
dteuk joo-un ទឹកជន់ flood
dteuk k'mao ទឹកខ្មៅ ink
dteuk k'meh ទឹកខ្មេះ vinegar
dteuk noam ទឹកនោម urine
dteuk om-beul ទឹកអំបិល perfume
dteuk op ទឹកអប់ salt water
dteuk p'nairk ទឹកភ្នែក tear (n)
dteuk peuk ទឹកផឹក drinking water
dteuk plai cher ទឹកផ្លែឈើ fruit juice
dteuk saap ទឹកសាប fresh water

dteuk t'lay-uk ទឹកធ្លាក់ waterfall

   s'raoch dteuk ស្រោចទឹក water (v)

dteuñ ទិញ buy

dteut-taa-gaa ទិដ្ឋាការ visa

dteuch តិច few

dti-dtee-un ទិទៀន criticize

dtoa-a-sa-naa-wa-day ទស្សនាវដ្ដី magazine

dtoa-ich តូច small

dtoa-un maong ទាន់ម៉ោង on time

dtoa-ut ទាត់ kick (v)

dtoah: k'mee-un dtoah គ្មានទោស innocent *(not guilty)*

   mee-un dtoah មានទោស guilty

dtoa-up ch'lorp ទ័ពឈ្លប guerrilla

dto តុ table

dtom-baañ តម្បាញ textile

dtom-born តបន region, district

dtom-lai (also **dom-lai**) តម្លៃ value, cost

   mee-un dtom-lai មានតម្លៃ valuable

dtom-naang តំណាង sample

dtom-naing តំណែង post, position

dtom-roo-ut តម្រួត police

dtoo ទូ cupboard

dtoo dteuk gork ទូទឹកកក refrigerator

dtoo kao-ao ទូខោអាវ wardrobe

dtoo see-a pou ទូសៀវភៅ bookcase

dtoo-dtou [also **(jee-a) dtoo-dtou**] (ជា)ទូទៅ general *(in general)*

dtook ទូក boat *(small)*

dtook g'daong ទូកក្ដោង sailboat

dtoo-a តួ body

dtoo-a aik តួឯក hero *(play, film)*

dtoo-a uk-sor តួអក្សរ letter, alphabet

dtoo-a yaang តួយ៉ាង example

dtoo-lee-ay ទូលាយ wide

dtoo-ra-dtoa-a ទូរទស្សន៍ television

dtoo-ra-sup ទូរស័ព្ទ telephone (n) (v)

dtoo-un ទន់ soft

dtoo-un-lay ទន្លេ river

dtoo-un-sai ទន្សាយ rabbit

dtoo-ung ទង flag

dtoo-ung daing ទងដែង brass

dtOOk ទុក keep, store, collect

dtOOm ទុំ ripe

dtOOm-bpairk ទុំពែក bald

dtOOm-bpay-ung bai joo ទុំពាំងបាយជូ grape

dtOOm-bpee-a ទុំពារ chew (v)

dtOOm-bpoa-a ទុំព័រ page

dtOOm-hOOm ទុំហំ size

dtOOm-nay ទុំនេរ empty, vacant

dtOOm-nee-um ទំនៀម custom

dtOOm-nerp ទំនើប modern

dtOOm-neuñ ទំនិញ merchandise

dtOOm-nOOp ទំនប់ dam, dike

dtOOm-ngoo-un ទម្ងន់ weight

dtOOm-rayt ទំរេត lie down

dtOOn ទុន capital *(money)*

dtor ត continue

dtor dtoo-ul តទល់ oppose

dtor soo តស៊ូ struggle (v)

dtor waa តវ៉ា protest, complain

dtor-dtay ទទេ empty

dtor-dteuk ទទឹក wet

dtor-dtoo-ul ទទួល accept; receive; welcome

dtor-dtoo-ul dtee-un ទទួលទាន eat *(formal)*

dtor-dtoo-ul koh dtrou ទទួលខុសត្រូវ take responsibility

dtorp តប answer (v)

dtou ទៅ go

dtou layng ទៅលេង visit (v)

dtra-bpay-ung ត្រពាំង pond

dtra-jay-uk ត្រជាក់ cool, cold

dtra-jee-uk ត្រចៀក ear

dtra-lop ត្រឡប់ return

dtraa ត្រា brand *(trademark)*

dt'ray ត្រី fish (n)

dtrayk-or ត្រេកអរ glad

dtreum dtrou ត្រឹមត្រូវ just *(fair)*

dtrou ត្រូវ have to, must; correct

dtrou-gaa ត្រូវការ need (v)

dtrong ត្រង់ straight

   dtrong nih ត្រង់នេះ right here

dtroo-ut ត្រួត inspect

dtrOOng ទ្រុង pen, enclosure, cage

dtrup ត្រាប់ imitate

dtuk-see តាក់ស៊ី taxi

dtung តាំង establish

dtung bpee តាំងពី since, starting from

e

ee-un អៀន shy

ee-un kloo-un អៀនខ្លួន embarrassed

eut ឥដ្ឋ brick

f

feem tort roop ហ្វីមថតរូប film *(for camera)*

g

ga-oo-ut ក្អួត vomit (v)

ga-ork ក្អក cough (v)

ga-sa-gum កសិកម្ម agriculture

gaa ការ job, work; married

   t'wer gaa ធ្វើការ work (v)

gaa hai-ee ការហើយ married

gaa joo-ay ការជួយ aid (n)

gaa seuk-saa ការសិក្សា education

gaa-boap bpruk កាបូបប្រាក់ wallet

gaa-rem ការ៉េម ice cream

gaa-ri-yaa-lai ការិយាល័យ office

gaa-ri-yaa-lai-ni-yOOm ការិយាល័យនិយម bureaucratism

gaa-sait កាសែត newspaper, magazine

   nay-uk gaa-sait អ្នកកាសែត journalist

gaam-ma-roak កាមរោគ venereal disease

gai-o កែវ glass (n)

gai-o yeut កែវយឹត binoculars

gairm កែម edge

gao-ay កៅអី chair

gao-soo កៅស៊ូ rubber, tire

gao កាវ glue

gao bpOOk moa-ut កោរពុកមាត់ shave (v)

gaot កោត admire

gart កើត born *(to be born)*; happen

   kaang gart ខាងកើត east

gart larng កើតឡើង happen, occur

gay គេ they

gay-a-na bpuk គណៈបក្ស party *(political)*

gay-a-neut-ta-saah គណិតសាស្ត្រ mathematics

gay-laa កីឡា sport

gay-ri-yah កិរិយា verb

g'baal ក្បាល head *(of body)*

g'boo-un hai ក្បួនហែ procession

g'bot ក្បត់ betray

g'bul កប៉ាល់ ship

g'bul hoh កប៉ាល់ហោះ airplane

g'daa ក្តារ board (n)

g'daa graal ក្តារក្រាល floor

g'daa kee-un ក្តារខៀន blackboard

g'daam ក្តាម crab

g'dao ក្តៅ hot

gee-loa-graam គីឡូក្រាម kilogram

gee-loa-mait គីឡូម៉ែត្រ kilometer

gee-up គាប squeeze

geu គឺ is; namely

geut គិត think, intend

geut t'lai គិតថ្លៃ charge (v)

geut-ta-yoo-ah កិត្តិយស honor

g'leun ក្លិន smell (n)

go-hok កុហក lie (v), tell lies

goa កូរ stir

goa គោ ox

goa-rOOp គោរព respect (v)

goa-um-bpee-a គាំពារ protect

goa-ut គាត់ he

goal bom-norng គោលបំណង goal, aim

goam គោម lantern

goan កូន child

goan bproh កូនប្រុស son

goan ngaa កូនង៉ា baby

goan ngait កូនងែត baby

goan sao កូនសៅ key

goan s'ray កូនស្រី daughter

goat-da-gum កូដកម្ម strike (n) *(labor)*

goh កោះ island

gok sok កក់សក់ shampoo

gom កុំ don't

gom joal កុំចូល no entry

gom-bplaing កំប្លែង funny

gom-bpool កំពូល top, summit

gom-bpOOng dtai កំពុងតែ in the process of

gom-bpong កំប៉ុង tin (n), can

gom-dao កំដៅ heat, temperature

gom-heung កំហឹង anger

gom-hoh កំហុស fault, mistake

gom-laich កម្ល្យាច frighten .

gom-loh កម្លោះ bachelor

gom-lung កម្លាំង energy; force, strength

   oh gom-lung អស់កម្លាំង exhausted *(tired)*

gom-nart កំណើត birth; origin

gom-not កំណត់ fix *(e.g., price)*

gom-nuñ កំណាញ់ stingy, mean

gom-raal grair dayk កម្រាលព្រៃដេក sheet

gom-rai កំប្រៃ profit

gon កុន film, movie

gon-daal កណ្ដាល middle

gon-dah កណ្ដាស់ sneeze (v)

gon-dee-a កណ្ដៀ. termite

gon-dol កណ្ដុរ mouse, rat

gon-dtayl កន្ទេល mat

gon-dtorp កន្ទប ' rag

gon-dtrai កន្ត្រៃ scissors

gon-lah កន្លះ half

   gon-lah maong កន្លះម៉ោង half an hour

gon-laing កន្លែង place (n)

gon-saing កន្សែង towel

gong កុង account *(bank)*

gong កង់ bicycle

gong-gaip កង្កែប frog

goñ-jer កញ្ជើ basket

goñ-jok កញ្ចក់ mirror

goñ-jop កញ្ចប់ package

goo គូ pair

goo-a dtai គួរតែ ought

goo-a sorm គួរសម polite; fair, just

goo-ah (t'wee-a) គោះ (ទ្វារ) knock (on a door)

goo-ee dtee-o គុយទាវ noodles

goo-ut គត់ exact

gOOk គុក jail

   duk gOOk ដាក់គុក to put in jail

   joa-up gOOk ជាប់គុក to be in jail

gOOm-bpoat គម្ពោត bush

gOOm-neut គំនិត thought, idea

gOOm-noo គំនូរ picture, painting

gOOm-nor គនរ pile (n)

gOOm-pay-a កុម្ភ: February

gOOm-roang gaa គម្រោងការណ៍ plan (n)

gOOm-roo គំរូ example

gOOm-rorp គំរប cover, lid

gOOn គុណ multiply

gOOn-na-toa-a គុណធម៌ virtue

gop កប់ bury

gor ក neck

gor dai កដៃ wrist

gor jerng កជើង ankle

gor គរ pile (n)

gor saang កសាង build (v)

gork កក frozen

gorl កល trick

gorng dtoa-up កងទ័ព army

gorng dtoa-up aa-gaah កងទ័ពអាកាស air force

got dtOOk កត់ទុក record (v), note

gra-bay ក្របី buffalo

gra-boap yoo-a ក្របូបយួរ handbag

gra-daah ក្រដាស paper

gra-horm ក្រហម red

    gaak-ga-baat gra-horm កាកបាតក្រហម Red Cross

    k'mai gra-horm ខ្មែរក្រហម Khmer Rouge

gra-soo-ung ក្រសួង ministry

gra-weul ក្រវិល earring

gra-wut ក្រវ៉ាត់ necktie

grah ក្រាស់ thick

grai-lairng ក្រៃលែង very

grair dayk ក្រែដេក bed

grao ក្រៅ outside

grao bpra-dtayh ក្រៅប្រទេស   abroad

grao-ee ក្រោយ   after

   kaang grao-ee ខាងក្រោយ   behind

graom ក្រោម   below, under

groa-ich ក្រូច   orange

groa-ich ch'maa ក្រូចឆ្មា   lemon

grom ក្រុម   group, team

grom hOOn ក្រុមហ៊ុន   firm (n) *(company)*

gror ក្រ   poor

gror-maa ក្រមា   scarf

guk-ga-daa កក្កដា   July

gum-beut កាំបិត   knife

gum-beut gao កាំបិតកោរ   razor

gum-joo-un-dar កាំជណ្ដើរ   stairs

gum-ma-gor កម្មករ   worker *(laborer)*

gum-ma-seut កម្មសិទ្ធិ   right of ownership

gum-plerng កាំភ្លើង   gun

gum-plerng klay កាំភ្លើងខ្លី   pistol

gum-plerng wairng កាំភ្លើងវែង   rifle

gun កាន់   hold

guñ-n'yaa កញ្ញា   September

gu-si-gor កសិករ   farmer, peasant

h

haam ហាម forbid

haam bpraam ហាមប្រាម suppress

haang ហាង shop

haang bai ហាងបាយ restaurant

haang gut day ហាងកាត់ដេរ tailor's shop

hai-ee ហើយ already

hail dteuk ហែលទឹក swim

haik ហែក tear, rip (v)

hait ហេតុ reason

   hait ay? ហេតុអ្វី? why?

   dao-ee hait nih ដោយហេតុនេះ for this reason

hait-gaa ហេតុការណ៍. event, situation

hao ហៅ to be called (*something*)

hao bpou ហៅប៉ៅ pocket

hao-raa-saah ហោរាសាស្ត្រ astrology

harm ហើម swell, swollen

heul (*also* **har**) ហើរ hot, spicy

heup ហិប box (n)

hoa ហូរ flow (v) (*river*)

hoap ហូប eat (*rural*)

hoh ហោះ fly (v)

hun ហាន់ slice (v)
hut ហាត់ practice

j

ja-raa-jor ចរាចរ traffic
jaa ចាំ yes *(female speaker)*
jaak jeuñ ចាកចេញ leave, depart
jaam ចាម Cham
jaan ចាន plate; bowl *(soup)*
jaan goo-ah ba-ray ចានគោះប៉ារី ashtray
jah ចាស់ old
jai ចាយ spend
jao ចោរ burglar, bandit, thief
jao ចៅ grandchild
jao bproh ចៅប្រុស grandson
jao dtoo-ut ចៅទ្វិត great-grandchild
jao s'ray ចៅស្រី granddaughter
jao-fai ចៅហ្វាយ boss
jao-fai kait ចៅហ្វាយខេត្ត governor *(provincial)*
jao-grom ចៅក្រម judge (n)
jayk ចេក banana

jayt-dta-naa ចេតនា intention

jee ជី fertilizer

jee-a ជា is

jee-ah wee-ung ជៀសវាង avoid

jee-ay dain ជាយដែន border *(frontier)*

jee-doan ជីដូន grandmother

jee-dtaa ជីតា grandfather

jee-un ចៀន fry

jee-ung ជាង than

jee-ung ជាង artisan

jee-ung cher ជាងឈើ carpenter

jee-ung gut day ជាងកាត់ដេរ tailor

jee-ung maa-seen ជាងម៉ាស៊ីន mechanic

jee-ung mee-ah ជាងមាស goldsmith

jee-ung plerng ជាងភ្លើង electrician

jee-ung tort roop ជាងថតរូប photographer

jee-ut ជាតិ nation

jee-ut nee-yOOm ជាតិនិយម nationalism

jee-wee-a-pee-up ជីវភាព way of life

jee-wee-a-saah ជីវសាស្ត្រ biology

jee-weut ជីវិត life

jeh ចេះ know *(how to do something)*

jerng ជើង foot, leg

jerng maa ជើងម៉ា bench

jeu-a ជឿ believe

jeun ចិន Chinese *(person)*

jeuñ-jarm ចិញ្ជើម eyebrow

jeuñ-jarm t'nol ចិញ្ជើមថ្នល់ sidewalk, pavement

jeuñ-jee-un ចិញ្ជៀន ring

jeut ចិត្ត heart

jeut ជិត near

ji-moo-ay ជាមួយ with

jih ជិះ ride (v)

joa-un ជាន់ story, floor; rank

joa-un graom ជាន់ក្រោម downstairs

joa-un ler ជាន់លើ upstairs

joa-up ជាប់ pass *(an exam)*

joal ចូល enter

joal jeut ចូលចិត្ត like (v)

joh ចុះ lower, descend, get off *(trains, etc.)*

jom-bung ចម្បាំង war

jom-gaa ចំការ plantation

jom-hai ចំហាយ steam (n)

jom-hoy ចំហុយ steam (v)

jom-loh ជម្លោះ row, quarrel

jom-lorng ចម្លង copy (v)

jom-nai ចំណាយ expenses; spend

jom-noo-un ចំនួន amount, number, quantity

jom-norng ចំណង ties (n), links

jom-nort yoo-un hoh ចំណតយន្តហោះ airport

jom-rarn ចំរើន progress (v)

jom-ree-ung ចម្រៀង song

jom-roh ចម្រុះ mixed

jong ចុង end

jong ចង់ want

jong baan ចង់បាន want

jong bom-pot ចុងបំផុត last *(final)*

jong-ao ចង្អោរ vomit (v)

jong-ee-ut ចង្អៀត narrow, crowded

jong-gaa ចង្កា chin

jong-gee-ung ចង្កៀង lamp *(electric)*

jong-geh ចង្កេះ waist

jong-geuh ចង្កឹះ chopsticks

jong-ol ចង្អុល point at

jong-wuk ចង្វាក់ rhythm

joo ជូរ sour

joo-a ជួរ row, line

joo-ah ជួស instead

joo-ah jOOl ជួសជុល fix, repair

joo-ay ជួយ help, assist

joo-uk (baa-ray) ជក់(បារី) smoke (cigarettes) (v)

joo-ul ជួល hire, employ, rent out

joo-ul ជល់ bump (v)

joo-un-dar yoang ជណ្ដើរយោង elevator

joo-un-gaal ជួនកាល sometimes

joo-uñ-jay-ung ជញ្ជាំង wall

joo-uñ-jeeng ជញ្ជីង scales *(for weighing)*

joo-un-jee-ut ជនជាតិ nationality

joo-uñ-joon ជញ្ជូន move *(something)*

joo-un pee-ah kloo-un ជនភៀសខ្លួន refugee

joo-up ជួប meet

joot ជូត wipe

jOOm-hee-un ជំហាន step, pace

jOOm-nee-uñ ជំនាញ skilled

jOOm-noo-ay ជំនួយ aid (n), assistance

jOOm-noo-uñ ជំនួញ business

   nay-uk jOOm-noo-uñ អ្នកជំនួញ businessman

jOOm-noon ជំនូន gift

jOOm-ngeu ជម្ងឺ illness

jOOm-ree-up soo-a ជំរាបសួរ greet; hello

jOOm-rOOm ជំរំ camp *(refugee)*

jop ចប់ finished

jor gao ជ័រការ glue

jor-jairk ជជែក argue

jorng ចង tie (v)

jorp ចប hoe (n)

jort ចត park (v)

j'ra-moh ច្រមុះ nose

j'ra-nain ច្រណែន jealous

j'raan jaol ច្រានចោល reject (v)

j'rarn ច្រើន many, much

j'reh ច្រេះ rust

j'ree-ung ច្រៀង sing

j'roo-uk ជ្រក់ pickle (v)

j'rook ជ្រូក pig

j'root s'rou ច្រូតស្រូវ harvest (v) *(rice)*

j'rork ច្រក lane

j'rOOl ជ្រុល exceed

juk ចាក់ inject; pour

juk sao ចាក់សោ lock (v)

jum ចាំ wait; remember

jum-baich ចាំបាច់ necessary

juñ ចាញ់ lose, be defeated

jup ចាប់ arrest (v)

jup jeut ចាប់ចិត្ត interested

jup p'darm ចាប់ផ្ដើម begin

jut jaing ចាត់ចែង arrange

k

kaan ខាន miss

kaan sa-aik ខានស្អែក the day after tomorrow

kaang ខាង side

kaang gart ខាងកើត east

kaang grao ខាងក្រៅ   outside

kaang ler ខាងលើ   on top of

kaang leuch ខាងលិច   west

kaang jerng ខាងជើង   north

kaang t'boang ខាងត្បូង   south

kai ខែ   month

kait ខេត្ត   province

kao ខោ   trousers

kao ao ខោអាវ   clothes, suit

kao ao k'nong ខោអាវក្នុង   underwear

k'bpoo-ah ខ្ពស់   high, tall

k'daa m'chooh ក្តារមឈូស   casket, coffin

k'day ក្តី   case *(legal)*

  gut k'day កាត់ក្តី   judge (v)

k'dtay-ah ខ្ទះ   frying pan

k'dteum sor ខ្ទឹមស   garlic

kee-a-ta-gor ឃាតករ   murderer

kee-a-ta-gum ឃាតកម្ម   murder

kee-mee គីមី   chemistry

kee-o ខៀវ   blue

kerñ ឃើញ   see

keung ខឹង   angry

k'jay ខ្ជី   light *(in color)*

k'jay-ah k'jee-ay ខ្ជះខ្ជាយ   waste (v)

k'jeul ខ្ជិល   lazy

k'jop ខ្ចប់ wrap

klaa ខ្លា tiger

klah ខ្លះ some, any

klaich ខ្លាច afraid

klao ខ្លៅ stupid

klay ខ្លី short

klay-ung ឃ្លាំង warehouse

klee-a ឃ្លា phrase, sentence

klee-un ឃ្លាន hungry

kloo-un (aing) ខ្លួន(ឯង) self

klung ខ្លាំង loud, strong

kluñ ខ្លាញ់ grease, fat (n)

k'maah ខ្មាស ashamed

k'mai ខ្មែរ Khmer, Cambodian *(person)*

k'mai gra-horm ខ្មែរក្រហម Khmer Rouge

k'mai graom ខ្មែរក្រោម Khmer Krom

k'mao ខ្មៅ black

k'mao dai ខ្មៅដៃ pencil

k'mayng ក្មេង child, children

k'mee-un គ្មាន not have, there isn't

k'moo-ay ក្មួយ nephew, niece

k'mOOm ឃ្មុំ bee

k'mung ខ្មាំង enemy

k'nar-ee ខ្នើយ pillow

k'nol *(also* **k'nao)** ខ្នុល jackfruit

k'nong ក្នុង in

k'norng ខ្នង back *(of body)*

k'nyay ខ្ញី ginger

k'nyom ខ្ញុំ I, me

koa-ich ខូច broken

koa-ich jeut ខូចចិត្ត broken-hearted

koa-sa-naa ឃោសនា advertise

koh ខុស wrong

koh ch'bup ខុសច្បាប់ illegal

kom ខំ hard-working, diligent

koo-a g'baal ខួរក្បាល brain

kOOn-na-pee-up គុណភាព quality

kra-wee ត្រវី wave (v) *(something)*

kree-a aa-son គ្រោអាសន្ន emergency

kreu-ung គ្រឿង equipment

kreu-ung a-long-gaa គ្រឿងអលង្ការ jewelry

kreu-ung bpruk គ្រឿងប្រាក់ silverware

kreu-ung dto dtoo គ្រឿងតុទូ furniture

kreu-ung layng គ្រឿងលេង toy

kreu-ung n'yee-un គ្រឿងញៀន drugs, narcotics

kreu-ung stoo-ung gom-dao គ្រឿងស្ទួងកំដៅ thermometer

kreu-ung yoo-un គ្រឿងយន្ត engine

kreu saa-s'naa គ្រីស្សាសនា Christianity

kroa-un dtai គ្រាន់តែ only

kroa-up ត្រាប់ nut *(edible)*

kroa-up baik dai ត្រាប់បែកដៃ grenade

kroa-up bpooch ត្រាប់ពូជ seed

kroa-up gum-plerng ត្រាប់កាំភ្លើង bullet

kroa-up meen ត្រាប់មីន mine (n) *(explosive)*

kroang គ្រោង plan (v); structure (n)

kroo គ្រូ teacher

kroo dtee-ay គ្រូទាយ astrologer, fortuneteller

kroo-a-saa គ្រួសារ family

kroo-ah t'nuk គ្រោះថ្នាក់ accident

krOOp kroa-un គ្រប់គ្រាន់ enough

krOOp krorng គ្រប់គ្រង administer

k'sai ខ្សែ line, rope

k'sai dai ខ្សែដៃ bracelet

k'sai gao-soo ខ្សែកៅស៊ូ rubber band

k'sai gor ខ្សែក necklace

k'sai gra-wut ខ្សែក្រវាត់ belt

k'sai loo-ah ខ្សែលួស cable *(wire)*

k'sai rorng-woa-ah ខ្សែរង្វាស់ measuring tape

k'sai root ខ្សែរូត zipper

k'sai s'baik jerng ខ្សែស្បែកជើង shoelace

k'sao-ee ខ្សោយ weak *(frail)*

k'teum baa-rung ខ្ទឹមបារាំង onion

k'tOOm ខ្ទម hut

kum ខាំ bite (v)

kwah   ខ្វះ   lack (v)

kwol   ខ្វល់   bothersome

kwuk   ខ្វាក់   blind (adj)

k'yol   ខ្យល់   wind, breeze

k'yorng   ខ្យង   oyster; shell

l

la-or   ល្អ   good, beautiful

laan   ឡាន   automobile, car

laan ch'noo-ul   ឡានឈ្នួល   bus

lao-see   ទ្រាស់   screw (n)

lark   លើក   pick something up, raise

larng   ឡើង   get up; go up; rise; get on *(trains etc.)*

lay-ew   ឡេវ   button

lay-kaa-ti-gaa   លេខាធិការ   secretary

lay-uk   លាក់   hide (v)

layk   លេខ   number

layk-kay-a-neut   លេខគណិត   arithmetic

layng   លេង   play (v)

layp   លេប   swallow

l'baing   ល្បែង   game

l'bay   ល្បី   famous

l'bay l'baañ   ល្បីល្បាញ   famous

l'beu-un ល្បៀន speed

lee លី to carry *(on the back or shoulders)*

lee-a seun hai-ee លាសិនហើយ goodbye

lee-ew លាវ Lao

lee-un លាន million

leet លីត្រ liter

ler លើ above, over

lerk lairng dtai លើកលែងតែ except (for)

lerk larng លើកឡើង lift (v)

leu ឮ hear

leu-un លឿន fast

leung លិង្គ penis

leuch លិច leak (v)

l'hong ល្ហុង papaya

l'kaon ល្ខោន play (n) *(theater)*

l'morm ល្មម enough

l'ngee-ich ល្ងាច afternoon *(late)*

loa-ha-tee-ut លោហធាតុ metal

loak លោក you *(to males)*

loak song លោកសង្ឃ monk

loak s'ray លោកស្រី you *(to older females)*

loak លោក world

loap លោភ greedy

loat លោត jump (v)

loo-ah លួស wire

loo-ich លួច steal

loo-uk លក់ sell

loon លូន crawl

lOOk លុក invade

lOOm-nou លំនៅ home

   dtee lOOm-nou ទីលំនៅ address (n)

lOOp លុប erase

lOOp jaol លុបចោល cancel (v)

lor ឡ oven

lor merl លមើល try out, try on

l'weeng ល្វីង bitter *(taste)*

m

ma-dtayh ម្ទេស chili

ma-dtayh plaok ម្ទេសផ្លោក green pepper

ma-haa sa-mot មហាសមុទ្រ ocean

ma-nOOh មនុស្ស person, human (n)

ma-nOOh-sa-toa-a មនុស្សធម៌ humanitarian

maa-seen ម៉ាស៊ីន machine

maa-seen dtra-jay-uk ម៉ាស៊ីនត្រជាក់ air conditioner

maa-seen tort roop ម៉ាស៊ីនថតរូប camera

mai ម៉ែ mother

mairn មែន real, genuine

mairn reu? មែនឬ? really?

mairn dtairn មែនទែន genuine

mait ម៉ែត្រ meter

maong ម៉ោង hour

may មេ headman

may dai មេដៃ thumb

may ree-un មេរៀន lesson

may-dtaa មេត្តា pity (n)

may-dtray-pee-up មេត្រីភាព friendship

may-om-bao មេអំបៅ butterfly

may-roak មេរោគ germ

may-saa មេសា April

may-tee-a-wee មេធាវី lawyer

mayk មេឃ sky

mayk-ga-raa មករា January

mayk-gOO-dtayh dtay-sa-jor មគ្គទេសក៍ទេសចរណ៍
   tourist guide

m'dai ម្តាយ mother

m'dorng ម្តង one time

mee មី egg noodles

mee-a មា uncle

mee-ah មាស gold

mee-un មាន have; wealthy

meeng មីង aunt

merl មើល look at, watch (v); read

meun មិន not

   meun ay dtay មិនអីទេ that's alright, never mind

   meun dail . . . មិនដែល ... never . . .

   meun sou . . . មិនសូរ៍ ... not very . . .

meun ម៉ឺន ten thousand

meut មិត្ត friend

m'hoap ម្ហូប food

m'jah ម្ចាស់ owner

m'jah p'dtay-ah ម្ចាស់ផ្ទះ landlord

m'jOOl ម្ជុល needle, pin

mi-to-naa មិថុនា June

mit-dta-pee-up មិត្តភាព friendship

m'noa-ah ម្នាស់ pineapple

moa-dtoa ម៉ូតូ motorcycle

moa-un មាន់ chicken

moa-ut មាត់ mouth

moo-ay មួយ one; a, an

moo-uk មួក hat

moo-ul ម្វិល twist (v)

moo-un dtee bpairt មន្ទីរពេទ្យ hospital

mooh មូស mosquito

mool មូល round

mool taan dtoa-up មូលដ្ឋានទ័ព military base

mOOk មុខ front; face

mOOk jee-a មុខជា probably

mOOk ra-bor មុខរបរ   occupation, profession

mOOn មុន   before; ago; former

mOOng មុង   mosquito net

m'pay ម្ភៃ   twenty

m'ree-um dai ម្រាមដៃ   finger

m'seul meuñ ម្សិលមិញ   yesterday

m'sao ម្សៅ   powder

m'sao doh t'mayñ ម្សៅដុះធ្មេញ   toothpaste

m'sao lee-up mOOk ម្សៅលាបមុខ   face powder

m'sao mee ម្សៅមី   flour

n

na-roo-uk និរក   hell

nah ណាស់   very

nay-uk bom-rar អ្នកបំរើ   servant

nay-uk deuk noa-um អ្នកដឹកនាំ   leader

nay-uk dom-naang អ្នកដំណាង   representative

nay-uk dom-nar អ្នកដំណើរ   passenger

nay-uk dtoah អ្នកទោស   prisoner

nay-uk geut loo-ee អ្នកគិតលុយ   cashier

nay-uk jOOm-nee-uñ gaa អ្នកជំនាញការ   expert (n)

nay-uk jOOm-ngeu អ្នកជម្ងឺ   patient

nay-uk jut gaa អ្នកចាត់ការ   manager

nay-uk mee-un អ្នកមាន   rich person, the rich

nay-uk naa អ្នកណា   who; anyone

nay-uk nay-saat dt'ray អ្នកនេសាទត្រី   fisherman

nay-uk ne-yoa-bai អ្នកនយោបាយ   politician

nay-uk roa-ut-dta-gaa អ្នករដ្ឋការ   government official

nay-uk som dtee-un អ្នកសុទាន   beggar

nay-uk s'rai អ្នកស្រែ   farmer, peasant

nay-uk yee-um អ្នកយាម   guard (n)

ne-yoa-bai នយោបាយ   politics

nee-a-li-gaa នាឡិការ   clock

nee-a-li-gaa roa នាឡិការរោទ៍   alarm clock

nee-a-dtee នាទី   minute

nee-um bun នាមបណ្ណ   business card

nee-um dtra-goal នាមត្រកូល   surname

neu-ay nai នឿយណាយ   bored

neuk នឹក   think of, think about

neuk p'dtay-ah នឹកផ្ទះ   homesick

neuk s'rok នឹកស្រុក   homesick

neung នឹង   will, shall; and; with

ni-moo-ay និមួយ   each

ni-ra-pay និរភ័យ   safety

ni-yee-ay និយាយ   speak, say

ni-yee-ay layng និយាយលេង   chat

ni-yoa-jeut និយោជិត   employee

ni-yoa-joo-uk និយោជក   employer

nih នេះ here

noam នោម urinate

nOOm នំ cake

nor-naa នរណា anyone; who?

nou នៅ at, be situated at, live

nou k'nong នៅក្នុង among

nou roo-a(h) នៅរស់ alive

nou sol នៅសល់ left over

   ...reu nou? ... ឬនៅ? ... yet?

nOOm-bpung នំបុ័ង bread

ngoot dteuk ងូតទឹក bathe

ngor-ngoo-ee dayk ងងុយដេក sleepy

n'yee-un ញៀន addict

n'yee-ut son-daan ញាតិសន្ដាន relative *(kin)*

n'yerh ញើស perspiration

n'yeuk-n'yoa-up ញឹកញាប់ frequently

n'yor-n'yeum ញញឹម smile (v)

n'yor-n'yoo-a ញញួរ hammer (n)

n'yum ញ៉ាំ eat *(colloquial)*

O

oa-bpOOk ឪពុក father

oa-bpOOk k'mayk ឪពុកក្មេក father-in-law

oa-bpOOk m'dai ឪពុកម្តាយ parents

oa-leuk ឪឡឹក watermelon

ok អក chest

om dtook អុំទូក row *(a boat)*

om-baoh អំបោស broom

om-bpee អំពី about, concerning

om-beul អំបិល salt

om-bpool plerng អំពូលភ្លើង lightbulb

om-bpou អំពៅ sugar cane

om-naich អំណាច power

on-daat អណ្តាត tongue

on-dait អណ្តែត float (v)

on-doang អណ្តូង well (n) *(water, oil)*

ong-gaa អង្គការ organization

ong-gaa sa-haa bpra-jee-a jee-ut អង្គការសហប្រជាជាតិ
    United Nations Organization

ong-goo-ee អង្គុយ sit

ong-gor អង្ករ husked rice

ong-reung អង្រឹង hammock

oo-ai អ៊ូអ៊ែ noisy

oo-ut អួត boast (v)

OO-bpa-suk ឧបសគ្គ obstacle

OO-dom-ga-dte ឧត្តមគតិ ideal (n)

OO-saa-ha-gum ឧស្សាហកម្ម industry

or-gOOn អរគុណ thank you

ot អត់ not, be without

ot bai អត់បាយ starving

ot mee-un អត់មាន not have, there isn't

ot too-un អត់ធន់ endure

p

pa-aim ផ្អែម sweet *(taste)*

pa-oam ផ្អើម bad *(food)*

pai ផែ harbor, pier

pain-dtee ផែនទី map

pain-gaa ផែនការណ៍ plan

p'daa sai ផ្ដាសាយ have a cold

p'dao ផ្ដៅ rattan

p'dtay-ah ផ្ទះ house

p'dtOOh ផ្ទុះ explode

pee-a-saa ភាសា language

pee-uk ភាគ part

pee-uk j'rarn ភាគច្រើន majority

pee-uk roy ភាគរយ percent

peuk ផឹក drink (v)

  kreu-ung peuk គ្រឿងផឹក beverage

p'gaa ផ្កា flower (n)

p'gaa s'bpay-ee ផ្កាស្ពៃ cauliflower

p'joo-a ភ្ជួរ   plow (v)

plah ផ្លាស់   change (v)

plah jeut ផ្លាស់ចិត្ត   change one's mind

plah p'doa ផ្លាស់ប្តូរ   change (v)

plah p'dtay-ah ផ្លាស់ផ្ទះ   move house

plai cher ផ្លែឈើ   fruit

playng ភ្លេង   music, song

plee-um ភ្លាម   as soon as, immediately

plee-ung ភ្លៀង   rain (n) (v)

plerng cheh ភ្លើងឆេះ   fire (n)

pleu ភ្លឺ   bright

pleuch ភ្លេច   forget

p'loo-uk ភ្លក់   taste (v)

plou ផ្លូវ   road, way *(route, path)*

plou ra-dtayh plerng ផ្លូវរទេះភ្លើង   railway

plou-gaa ផ្លូវការ   formal

   grao plou-gaa ក្រៅផ្លូវការ   informal, unofficial

p'naik ផ្នែក   part, section

p'nairk ភ្នែក   eye

p'nay-uk ngee-a ភ្នាក់ងារ   official (n)

p'noa-ul ភ្នាល់   bet (v)

p'noo ផ្នូរ   grave (n)

p'nOOm ភ្នំ   hill, mountain

p'nyar ផ្ញើ   send

p'nyay-uk ភ្ញាក់   awake; surprised

p'nyee-o ភ្ញៀវ visitor, guest

poa-cha-nee-ya-taan ភោជនីយដ្ឋាន restaurant

poo-ay ភួយ blanket

poo-uk ភក់ mud

poom ភូមិ village

　nay-uk poom អ្នកភូមិ villager

poom-i-saah ភូមិសាស្ត្រ geography

pol ផល effect (n)

p'saa ផ្សារ market

p'saing ផ្សែង smoke (n)

p'sayng ផ្សេង different

p'sayng p'sayng ផ្សេង ៗ various

p'seut ផ្សិត mushroom

r

ra-bee-up របៀប system

ra-boh របស់ of, belonging to; thing

ra-boo-ah របួស wound, wounded

ra-borng របង fence

ra-borp របប system

ra-bpeul ra-bpoach របិលរប៉ូច naughty

ra-dou រដូវ season; menstrual period

　ra-dou g'dao រដូវក្តៅ hot season

ra-dou plee-ung រដូវភ្លៀង rainy season
ra-dou ra-ngee-a រដូវរងា cool season

ra-dtayh រទេះ cart
ra-dtayh gong រទេះកង់ bicycle
ra-haik រហែក torn
ra-lay-uk រលាក់ bumpy
ra-loo-ay រលួយ bad, rotten *(fruit)*
ra-lOOng រលុង loose *(fitting)*
ra-lork រលក wave *(in the sea)*
ra-moa-ah រមាស់ itch (v)
ra-naa រណារ saw (n)
ra-nay-ung រនាំង curtain
ra-nee-ut រនៀត xylophone
ra-noa-ah រនាស់ rake (n)
ra-nOOk រនុក bolt (n)
duk ra-nOOk ដាក់រនុក bolt (v)
ra-ngee-a រងា cold (adj)
ra-see-ul រសៀល afternoon *(early)*
ra-wee-ung រវាង between
ra-woo-ul រវល់ busy
ree-ay gaa រាយការណ៍ report (v)
ree-ich-tee-a-nee រាជធានី capital city *(of a kingdom)*
ree-un រៀន learn, study
ree-un jop រៀនចប់ graduate (v)
ree-up រាប flat

ree-up s'mar រាបស្មើ smooth, flat

ree-up រៀប prepare

ree-up jom រៀបចំ arrange, prepare

ree-up gaa រៀបការ get married

ree-up roy រៀបរយ tidy

rerh រើស choose

reu ឬ or

reu-say ឫស្សី bamboo

reu-ung រឿង story

roak រោគ disease

roak dayk neung s'ray រោគដេកនឹងស្រី venereal disease

roak klaich dteuk រោគឆ្កាចទឹក rabies

roak kun leu-ung រោគខាន់លឿង jaundice

roak ra-lee-uk t'larm រោគរលាកថ្លើម hepatitis

roak s'wai រោគស្វាយ syphilis

roang រោង hall, large building

   roang gon រោងកុន cinema

   roang jee-ung រោងជាង workshop

   roang jort laan រោងចតឡ្បាន garage *(at house)*

   roang juk រោងចក្រ factory

   roang juk dom-baañ រោងចក្រតម្បាញ textile mill

   roang l' kaon រោងល្ខោន theater

   roang pee-up-yoo-un រោងភាពយន្ត cinema

roa-ul រាល់ every

roa-up រាប់ count (v)

roa-ut-a-pi-baal រដ្ឋភិបាល government

roo-ee រុយ fly (n) *(insect)*

roo-um រួម add, join

roo-um dtay-ung រួមទាំង including

roo-up roo-um k'nee-a រួបរួមគ្នា unite

roo-ut រត់ run

roo-ut yoo-un រថយន្ត motor vehicle

roong រូង hole; cave

roop រូប picture

roop ree-ung រូបរាង shape

roop tort រូបថត photograph

rOO-see រុស្ស៊ី Russia

rOOk ree-un រុករាន invade

rOOm-kaan រខាន bothersome

rOOm-leuk រំលឹក remind

rOOm-loo-ut រំលត់ extinguish

   kreu-ung rOOm-loo-ut plerng គ្រឿងរំលត់ភ្លើង fire

   extinguisher

rork រក look for

rork kerñ រកឃើញ find

rork see រកស៊ី earn a living

rorng-woa-un រង្វាន់ prize

roy រយ hundred

rup-rorng រ៉ាប់រង guarantee (v)

S

sa-aat ស្អាត beautiful, clean, neat

sa-aat baat ស្អាតបាត tidy

sa-dtrou សត្រូវ enemy

sa-eut ស្អិត sticky

sa-haa roa-ut aa-may-rik សហរដ្ឋអាមេរិក United States

sa-maa-gOOm សមាគម association

sa-maa-jeuk សមាជិក member

   sa-maa-jeuk sa-pee-a សមាជិកសភា member of
   parliament

sa-mai សម័យ era

sa-mot សមុទ្រ sea

sa-op ស្អប់ hate (v)

sa-oy ស្អុយ stink (v)

sa-paa jee-ut សភាជាតិ parliament

saa-bpoo សាប៊ូ soap

saa-gol-loak សាកលលោក world

saa-gol wit-yee-a-lai សាកលវិទ្យាល័យ university

saa-kaa សាខា branch *(office)*

saa-laa សាលា hall *(pavilion)*

saa-laa gut k'day សាលាកាត់ក្ដី court *(law)*

saa-laa ree-un សាលារៀន school

saa-ra-moo-un-dtee សារមន្ទីរ museum

saa-sa-naa សាសនា religion

saap សាប sow (v); fresh *(water)*

saich សាច់ meat, flesh

saich goa សាច់គោ beef

saich grork សាច់ក្រក sausage

saich j'rook សាច់ជ្រូក pork

saich moa-un សាច់មាន់ chicken

sain សែន hundred thousand

sao-mao សាវម៉ាវ rambutan

sarm សើម humid

say-haa សីហា August

say-ray-pee-up សេរីភាព freedom

sayt-ta-geuch សេដ្ឋកិច្ច economy

sayt-ta-saah សេដ្ឋសាស្ត្រ economics

s'baik ស្បែក skin

s'baik jerng ស្បែកជើង shoe

s'baik sut ស្បែកសត្វ leather

s'bot ស្បថ swear

s'bpee-un ស្ពាន bridge

s'dai ស្ដាយ regret (v)

s'daich ស្ដេច king

s'darng ស្ដើង thin *(things)*

s'doh ស្ដោះ spit

s'dup ស្ដាប់ listen

    s'dup meun baan ស្ដាប់មិនបាន I can't hear

s'dup leu ស្ដាប់ឮ hear

s'dum ស្ដាំ right *(side)*

see ស៊ី eat *(vulgar)*

see-kloa ស៊ីក្លូ cyclo

see-a pou សៀវភៅ book (n)

see-daa ស៊ីដា AIDS (SIDA)

seh សេះ horse

seu-la-bpa សិល្បៈ art

seu-la-bpa-gor សិល្បករ artist

seup-bpa-gum សិប្បកម្ម handicraft

seut សិត comb (v)

seut-dti សិទ្ធិ right (n)

  seut-dti ma-nOOh សិទ្ធិមនុស្ស human rights

s'koa-ul ស្គាល់ know *(people, places)*

s'kor ស្ករ sugar

s'korm ស្គម thin *(people)*

s'laak ស្លាក label

s'laap ស្លាប wing

s'laap bpree-a ស្លាបព្រា spoon

slee-uk bpay-uk ស្លៀកពាក់ wear *(clothes)*

s'leuk cher ស្លឹកឈើ leaf

s'loat ស្លូត gentle

s'loat la-or ស្លូតល្អ good-natured

s'maan ស្មាន guess (v), suppose

s'mao ស្មៅ grass

s'mar (neung) ស្មើ (នឹង) equal (to); level

s'muk jeut ស្ម័គ្រចិត្ត volunteer (v)

s'nar ស្នើ advise, recommend

s'ngee-um ស្ងៀម silent

s'ngut ស្ងាត់ quiet

so-pee-up bo-roh សុភាពបុរស gentleman

soam សូម please

soam dtoah សូមទោស excuse me

soan សូន្យ zero

soch-ja-reut សុច្ចរិត honest

sok សក់ hair

sok សុខ happy

sok-ka-pee-up សុខភាព health

som សុំ ask *(for something)*

som dtoah សុំទោស; សូមទោស apologize

som soo-a សុំសួរ ask *(a question)*

som dtee-un សុំទាន beg

som-aat សំអាត clean (v)

som-bork សំបក peel (n)

som-bot សំបុត្រ letter *(mail)*; bill; certificate

som-bpoo-ut សពត់ skirt

som-kun សំខាន់ important

som-lay សំឡី cotton wool

som-layng សំឡេង voice, sound

som-lee-uk bom-bpay-uk សំលៀកបំពាក់ clothes

som-lup សម្លាប់ kill, murder

som-naang សំណាង luck

   k'mee-un som-naang គ្មានសំណាង unlucky

som-noo-a សំណួរ question (n)

som-nook សំណូក bribe (n)

som-nor សំណ lead (n) *(metal)*

som-norng សំណង់ building

som-ngut សម្ងាត់ secret (adj)

som-pee-ah សម្ភាសន៍ interview (n)

   t'wer som-pee-ah ធ្វើសម្ភាសន៍ interview (v)

som-raak សម្រាក rest (v); stay at a hotel

som-raal goan សំរាលកូន give birth to

som-raam សំរាម garbage

som-roo-ul សម្រួល adjust

som-rOOm សមរម្យ appropriate, suitable

som-rup សម្រាប់ for

son-daik សណ្ដែក bean

son-daik day សណ្ដែកដី peanut

son-dti-pee-up សន្តិភាព peace

soñ-jee-ut សញ្ជាតិ nationality

song សង់ build (v)

song-dti-mait សង់ទីម៉ែត្រ centimeter

song-gayt សង្កេត observe, notice

song-gOOm សង្គម society

song-keum សង្ឃឹម   hope (v), expect

song-kree-um សង្គ្រាម   war

son-som សន្សំ   save

son-ta-gee-a សណ្ឋាគារ   hotel

son-yaa សន្យា   promise (v)

soo-a សួរ   ask

soo-a jom-lar-ee សួរចម្លើយ   interrogate

soo-un សួន   park, garden

soo-un ch'baa សួនច្បារ   park, garden

soo-un sut សួនសត្វ   zoo

soo-ut សួត   lung

sook សូក   bribe (v)

sop-bai សប្បាយ   glad, happy, well

sop t'ngai nih សព្វថ្ងៃនេះ   nowadays

sor-say សរសេរ   write

sorm សម   suitable, fitting; fork

sot-saat សុទ្ធសាធ   pure

s'ra ស្រៈ   vowel

s'ra-luñ ស្រឡាញ់   love (v)

s'ra-maoch ស្រមោច   ant

s'raa ស្រា   alcohol *(liquor)*

s'raal ស្រាល   light *(in weight)*

s'rai ស្រែ   rice field

s'raik ស្រែក   shout, scream

s'rao j'ree-o ស្រាវជ្រាវ research (v)

s'raom ស្រោម envelope

s'raom un-naa-mai ស្រោមអនាម័យ condom

s'raom jerng ស្រោមជើង sock

s'raom som-bot ស្រោមសំបុត្រ envelope

s'ray ស្រី female

s'rayk dteuk ស្រេកទឹក thirsty

s'roh ស្រស់ fresh

s'rok ស្រុក country, district

s'rok s'rai ស្រុកស្រែ countryside

s'roo-ay · ស្រួយ fragile

s'roo-ul ស្រួល easy, convenient

s'rou ស្រូវ unhusked rice

s'taan dtoot ស្ថានទូត embassy

s'taan-na-gaa ស្ថានការណ៍ situation

s'taan-nee ស្ថានីយ station

ster dtai ស្ទើរតែ almost, nearly

sung សាំង gas, gasoline

suñ-n'yaa សញ្ញា sign (n)

sut សត្វ animal

sut la-eut សត្វល្អិត insect

s'waa ស្វា monkey

s'wai ស្វាយ mango

t

tor-nee-a-gee-a ធនាគារ bank

taah ថាស tray

tai ថៃ Thai

tai dtoa-um ថៃទាំ care for

tai ray-uk-saa ថៃរក្សា care for

taok ថោក cheap

tarp ថើប kiss (v)

t'baañ ត្បាញ weave

t'boang ត្បូង gem, precious stone

tee-ut aa-gaah ធាតុអាកាស weather

t'lai ថ្លៃ price, cost

t'lai ch'noo-ul ថ្លៃឈ្នួល fare

t'lai joal ថ្លៃចូល admission *(price)*

t'lai t'laa ថ្លៃថ្លា valuable

   dtor t'lai តថ្លៃ bargain (v)

t'larm ថ្លើម liver

t'lay-uk ធ្លាក់ fail *(an exam)*

t'lee-a s'mao ធ្លាស្មៅ lawn

t'loa-up ធ្លាប់ used to, formerly

t'loap neung ធ្លាប់នឹង accustomed (to)

t'may ថ្មី new

t'may t'may nih ថ្មី ៗ នេះ recently

t'mayñ ធ្មេញ tooth, teeth

t'mor ថ្ម battery; rock, stone

t'nar ធ្នើរ shelf

t'nuk ថ្នាក់ grade, class

t'num ថ្នាំ medicine

t'num bpOOl ថ្នាំពុល poison

t'num gok ថ្នាំកក់ shampoo

t'num joo-uk ថ្នាំជក់ tobacco

t'num layp ថ្នាំលេប tablet

t'num lee-up ថ្នាំលាប paint

t'ngai ថ្ងៃ day

t'ngai chOOp som-raak ថ្ងៃឈប់សម្រាក holiday

t'ngai gart ថ្ងៃកើត birthday

t'ngai dtrong ថ្ងៃត្រង់ midday

t'ngoo-un ធ្ងន់ heavy; serious *(illness)*

toa ថូ vase

toa-ut ធាត់ fat (adj)

toa-um-a-daa ធម្មតា usually

tom ធំ big; aunt *(older sister of mother or father)*

tom som-barm ធំសម្បើម huge

tong ថង់ bag

tong gra-daah ថង់ក្រដាស paper bag

too-un ធ្ងន់ endure

toop ធូប incense

tOOng ធុង bucket, tank

tOOñ ធុញ annoyed

tOOñ dtroa-un ធុញទ្រាន់ bored

tort aik-ga-saa ថតឯកសារ photocopy (v)

tort roop ថតរូប photograph (v)

tort som-layng ថតសម្លេង record (v) *(sounds)*

toy ថយ go back, reverse

tung ថាំង bucket

t'wayh bpra-haih ធ្វេសប្រហែស careless

t'wee-a ទ្វារ gate

t'wer ធ្វើ do, make

t'wer bpee ធ្វើពី made of

t'wer dom-nar ធ្វើដំណើរ travel (v)

t'wer koh ធ្វើខុស make a mistake

t'yoong ធ្យូង charcoal

u

uk-gee-sa-nee អគ្គីសនី electricity

uk-sor អក្សរ alphabet, letter

um-baañ meuñ អម្បាញ់មិញ just now

ung អាំង roast (v)

un-dark អណ្ដើក turtle, tortoise

uñ-jerñ អញ្ជើញ invite (v); please . . .
ut-dtraa អត្រា rate

W

wain dtaa វែនតា glasses *(spectacles)*
wairng វែង long *(size)*
way-ung វាំង palace
wee-a វា it
wee-a-sa-naa វាសនា fate
wee-ay វាយ beat (v), hit
wee-ay duk-dtee-loa វាយដាក់ទីឡ type (v)
wi-nee-a-dtee វិនាទី second *(unit of time)*
wi-sa-ma-gaal វិស្សមកាល vacation
wi-s'wa-gor វិស្វករ engineer
wi-s'wa-gum វិស្វកម្ម engineering
wi-tay វិថី road, street
wi-tee វិធី way *(method, means)*
wit-yee-a-saah វិទ្យាសាស្ត្រ science
wit-yOO វិទ្យុ radio
woa-ah វាស់ measure (v)
woa-ut វត្ត temple, *wat*
woo-ung mool វង់មូល circle
woo-ung playng វង់ភ្លេង band *(music)*

wun-nah វណ្ណ: class *(social)*
wup-bpa-toa-a វប្បធម៌ culture

y

yaang យ៉ាង like; kind, type; way
   yaang maych? យ៉ាងម៉េច how?
   yaang nih យ៉ាងនេះ like this
yee hao យីហោ brand *(trademark)*
yee-ay យាយ grandmother
yee-un jOOm-nih យានជំនិះ vehicle
yerng យើង we, us
yerng k'ñom យើងខ្ញុំ we, us
yeut យឺត late; slow
yoa-bol យោបល់ advice, opinion
yoa-nee យោនី vagina
yoa-tee-a យោធា soldier
yoak យក take
yoo យូរ a long time
yoo-a យួ carry *(in the hands)*
yoo-ul យល់ understand, think
yoo-ul bprorm យល់ព្រម agree (with, to); agreed
yoo-ul koh យល់ខុស misunderstand
yoo-un hoh យន្តហោះ airplane

yOOm យំ cry *(tears)*

yOOp យប់ night

   yOOp meuñ យប់មិញ last night

yOOt-dta-toa-a យុត្តិធម៌ justice

APPENDIXES

Appendix 1

NUMBERS

1	moo-ay	មួយ
2	bpee	ពីរ
3	bay	បី
4	boo-un	បួន
5	bprum	ប្រាំ
6	bprum moo-ay	ប្រាំមួយ
7	bprum bpee *(formal)*	ប្រាំពីរ
	or bprum bpeul *(colloquial)*	
8	bprum bay	ប្រាំបី
9	bprum boo-un	ប្រាំបួន
10	dop	ដប់
11	dop moo-ay *(formal)*	ដប់មួយ
	or moo-ay don-dop	មួយដណ្ដប់
	(colloquial)	
12	dop bpee	ដប់ពីរ
	or bpee don-dop	ពីរដណ្ដប់

13	dop bay	ដប់បី
	or bay don-dop	បីដណ្ដប់
14	dop boo-un	ដប់បួន
	or boo-un don-dop	បួនដណ្ដប់
15	dop bprum	ដប់ប្រាំ
	or bprum don-dop	ប្រាំដណ្ដប់
16	dop bprum moo-ay	ដប់ប្រាំមួយ
	or bprum moo-ay don-dop	ប្រាំមួយដណ្ដប់
17	dop bprum bpee	ដប់ប្រាំពីរ
	or dop bprum-bpeul	
	or bprum-bpeul don-dop	ប្រាំពីរដណ្ដប់
18	dop bprum bay	ដប់ប្រាំបី
	or bprum-bay don-dop	ប្រាំបីដណ្ដប់
19	dop bprum boo-un	ដប់ប្រាំបួន
	or bprum boo-un don-dop	ប្រាំបួនដណ្ដប់
20	m'pay	ម្ភៃ
21	m'pay moo-ay	ម្ភៃមួយ
22	m'pay bpee	ម្ភៃពីរ
23	m'pay bay	ម្ភៃបី
24	m'pay boo-un	ម្ភៃបួន
30	saam seup	សាមសិប
31	saam seup moo-ay	សាមសិបមួយ

32	saam seup bpee	សាមសិបពីរ
40	sai seup	សែសិប
50	haa seup	ហាសិប
60	hok seup	ហុកសិប
70	jeut seup	ចិតសិប
80	bpait seup	ប៉ែតសិប
90	gao seup	កៅសិប
100	(moo-ay) roy	(មួយ)រយ
101	roy moo-ay	រយមួយ
110	roy dop	រយដប់
200	bpee roy	ពីររយ
300	bay roy	បីររយ
1000	(moo-ay) bpoa-un	(មួយ)ពាន់
10,000	(moo-ay) meun	(មួយ)ម៉ឺន
100,000	(moo-ay) sain	(មួយ)សែន
1,000,000	(moo-ay) lee-un	(មួយ)លាន

Appendix 2

DAYS, MONTHS, SEASONS

DAYS

Sunday   t'ngai aa-dteut   ថ្ងៃអាទិត្យ

Monday   t'ngai juŋ   ថ្ងៃចន្ទ

Tuesday   t'ngai ong-gee-a   ថ្ងៃអង្គារ

Wednesday   t'ngai bpOOt   ថ្ងៃពុធ

Thursday   t'ngai bpra-hoa-a   ថ្ងៃព្រហស្បតិ៍

Friday   t'ngai sok   ថ្ងៃសុក្រ

Saturday   t'ngai sao   ថ្ងៃសៅរ៍

MONTHS

January   mayk-ga-raa   មករា

February   gOOm-pay-a   កុម្ភៈ

March   mee-nee-a   មីនា

April   may-saa   មេសា

May   OO-sa-pee-a   ឧសភា

June   mi-to-naa   មិថុនា

July   guk-ga-daa   កក្កដា

August   say-haa   សីហា

September   kañ-n'yaa   កញ្ញា

October   dto-laa   តុលា

November   weuch-a-gaa   វិច្ឆិកា

December   t'noo   ធ្នូ

SEASONS

hot season   ra-dou k'dao   រដូវក្តៅ

rainy season   ra-dou plee-ung   រដូវភ្លៀង

cool season   ra-dou ra-ngee-a   រដូវរងា

Appendix 3

CAMBODIAN PROVINCES

Note that province names are frequently preceded by the word
kait (ខេត្ត), the Cambodian for "province."

Battambang   but-dtom-borng   ប្រាត់តំបង

Kampong Cham   gom-bpoo-ung jaam   កំពង់ចាម

Kampong Chhnang   gom-bpoo-ung ch'nung   កំពង់ឆ្នាំង

Kampong Speu   gom-bpoo-ung speu   កំពង់ស្ពឺ

Kampong Thom   gom-bpoo-ung tom   កំពង់ធំ

Kampot   gom-bport   កំពត

Kandal   gon-daal   កណ្ដាល

Koh Kong   goh gong   កោះកុង

Kratié   gra-jeh   ក្រចេះ

Mondulkiri   mOOn-doo-ul-gi-ree   មណ្ឌលគីរី

Prey Veng   bpray-ee wairng   ព្រៃវែង

Pursat   bpoa-sut   ពោធិសាត់

Ratanakiri   roat-ta-na-gi-ree   រតនៈគីរី

Siem Reap   see-um-ree-up   សៀមរាប
Stung Treng   steung dtraing   ស្ទឹងត្រែង
Svay Rieng   swai-ree-ung   ស្វាយរៀង
Takéo   dtaa-gai-o   តាកែវ

Appendix 4

CAMBODIAN ALPHABET

Consonants (with subscript forms)

ក g	ខ k	គ g	ឃ k	ង ng
ច j	ឆ ch	ជ j	ឈ ch	ញ ny/ñ
ដ d	ឋ t	ឌ d	ឍ t	ណ n
ត dt	ថ t	ទ dt	ធ t	ន n
ប b	ផ p	ព bp	ភ p	ម m
យ y	រ r	ល l	វ w	
ស s	ហ h	ឡ l	អ (-)	

Vowels

-ꄱ	◌	◌	◌	◌
-ah/-ee-a	-e/-i̧	-ay/-ee	-eu	-eu

◌	◌	◌
-o/-OO	-oa/-oo	-oo-a

ເ◌	ເ◌	ເ◌	ເ◌
-ar/er	-eu-a	-ee-a	-ay

◌	◌	ເ◌	ເ◌
-ai/-air	-ai/-ay-ee	-ao/-oa	-ao/-ou

◌	◌	◌	◌
-om/-OOm	-om/-OOm	-um/-oa-um	-ah/ay-ah

◌	ເ◌	ເ◌
-oh/-OOh	-eh/ih	-ah/-oo-ah

For a detailed description of the Cambodian writing system, see *Cambodian System of Writing and Beginning Reader* by Franklin Huffman (Yale University Press, 1970). *Colloquial Cambodian* (Routledge, 1995) by David Smyth includes a step-by-step introduction to reading and writing Cambodian.

— NOTES —

— NOTES —

— NOTES —